'By chance, some years ago I was persuaded
by the name of Joey Howard. For over ar
masterclass of creative comedy, razor shar, ... ---- - ,
mesmerised the audience. I became a devoted fan. Both myself and my
family have seen him work many times. A rare undiscovered talent that
should have hit national stardom years ago!'

Norman Collier

'I was privileged to share the stage with Joey Howard for over two
years, working the holiday camp circuit, theatres and corporates in the
UK and '5 star' holiday venues throughout Europe. I learnt so much
from this skilled craftsman, who had honed his comedy box of tricks
over many years. He genuinely made me laugh at every gig where I
shared the stage with him. He could turn a tough venue into a great
venue. I bathed in the joy and laughter of the audiences. I continue to
admire and respect the natural talent of my very funny comedy act
partner, who remains one of my closest friends.'

John Ainsley

'Having just completed fifty years as a theatrical agent I can write with
some authority on the comedian Joey Howard. I have represented him
for some twenty years and can confirm that Joey is a dedicated and
highly talented entertainer. Over this time I have received countless
endorsements from venues, managements and indeed the general
public. He is, in my opinion a true variety performer. Having booked
him for shows throughout the UK and abroad; he has never failed to
impress. A really funny professional man, who it has been a joy to
represent.'

Paul Bridson (Paul Bridson Productions)

Joey who?

Joey Howard

A Memoir

Hird Publications

First Published in 2019
by Hird Publications

ISBN 978-1-9162993-0-6

The moral right of Joey Howard to be identified as the author of this
work has been asserted in accordance with the Copyright Designs and
Patents Act 1988

Hird Publications
81 Bernadette Avenue
Anlaby Common
Hull HU4 7BQ

Design and set Andrew Jackson
Printed by Central Printing Services
University of Hull

Cover picture by Jimmy Marshall Photography (1981)

For Lynda

Foreword

I first met Joey in 2011 in the Minerva pub in Hull. His wife Lynda and I had been rehearsing a play there and she introduced us. Within minutes he was making me laugh – and I've been laughing with him ever since. Several years later he told me he'd finished writing his autobiography and was looking for an editor. I'd edited a variety of books in the past but never done an autobiography so I was interested in reading it with a view to becoming his editor.

Little did I know then what I was letting myself in for!

Joey turned up at my house in February 2017 with a bulging folder, gave me a resume of what was in it, regaled me with stories of his life for a couple of hours, enjoyed several cups of coffee and half of my lemon loaf and left me with the folder. I read it from cover to cover the next day. It was chaotic! Disorganised, unstructured, not very chronological (apart from his childhood memories) and the technical elements were enough to make a retired English teacher weep!

However, these random tales of a drummer turned comedian were fascinating. It was socially and historically interesting, varied, detailed, visual, full of pathos and charm – and above all, it was hilarious!

I decided I would become his editor and there followed a year of bi-weekly Monday mornings sitting with Joey and his wayward twenty five 'chapters'. We discussed every one of them in detail and his story began to emerge, to become a worthwhile project and a very readable, entertaining autobiography. And we were still laughing!

I'm so glad I took it on and I'm proud to have been a part of *Joey Who?*

Nora Jones November 2019

Acknowledgements

I would like to thank my good friend John Ainsley for his support and laughter over the past 25 years and for his profound understanding of the all highs and lows in this industry we call show business.

To my dear friend Mike Lodge, a true professional, a master of his craft as a performer. Thank you for all the happy memories we have shared together over the years.

To my two sons, Simon and Joey who have both witnessed my ambitious struggles and career moves, some of which they have been involved in. I think they have forgiven me. I thank you both.

I would like to thank Nodge Jones, my editor who over the last three years with her patience, confidence, determination and guidance, helped me to finish this book. Also my express gratitude goes to Andrew Jackson for his skill and expertise in making my book look like a real one.

To Paul Bridson. An agent with impeccable taste for spotting the right talent at the right time. When he spotted me his watch stopped! I have paid him 15% for the last 25 years keeping him in the life style to which he is accustomed. He taught me that money isn't everything. Thank you Paul.

Last but not least, Lynda, who for more than forty years has supported me in every madcap scheme I have ventured into. And for being my best friend.

Contents

THE SECOND BEGINNING

Prologue

Well, there you are. Is it April 1ˢᵗ? Is there a shower outside? Have you run quickly into this shop out of the rain? Does your umbrella need a shake? April fool! Got you! Well, obviously, you now have both hands free and the title of *Joey Who?* together with my face on the cover, has caught your eye and you've opened the first page to browse the inner mind of a comedian.

I've been threatening to put pen to paper for the last two years. However, what with watering plants, cutting the grass, shopping at Lidl and accumulating speeding points on the highways and by-ways of Great Britain, somehow writing a book was my last priority. But at last, after dusting and vacuuming the fluff from under the bed and hanging a full line of washing out, I decided it was time to make a start.

It's now 11.45pm. I've just watched two Channel 4 films and now, tonight's the night. I don't know how many words I'll write, but writing is better than lying in bed awake until 5am, because your head's a shed with ideas and thoughts of the past. I'll write about the laughs, the disasters and failures I've encountered while parking my bike on this planet of ours. So let's get it down on paper...

... just off outside for a fag first – I'll be back, however, to indulge in this 'not to be missed' autobiography of 'JOEY WHO?'...

I can hear you wondering, is it Joe Loss, the famous bandleader – is it him? Or Joe Bugner, the famous boxer? Or, could it be Joe Longthorne the famous singer? Even Joey the famous budgie who won The British Canary Karaoke Awards 2011? No, it's JOEY HOWARD the *not* so famous comedian.

Who? Yes I knew you would ask that. I'm surprised that you, as a reader, would have enough interest to read this far but it's probably because you're waiting for your partner who is in WH.Smiths next door, perusing Mary Berry's best seller *I've Got A Bun In The Oven.*

Well, thank you for reading this far about an unknown comedian. I have forty five years of experience, treading the boards. I know – it sounds like I'm a builder, stamping on rotten joists, looking for dry rot in old houses. Well for all you non-'lovies' out there in Normal Land, 'treading the boards' is a theatrical term for working every public house, club, theatre and shithole in the country. That would just about earn you enough money to pay your agent's commission, possibly buy a porkpie, and fill up with enough diesel, ready to travel to the next gig like a lamb to the slaughter. Some of us have never made it. I've been a hundred miles away from stardom; some people say I was on another planet. However, I have worked solidly as a performer for the last forty five years up and down that rocky road.

I'm still wondering... why are you reading this book? Are you standing in a charity shop pondering whether to spend 50 pence on a discarded book after getting to page two? Have I grabbed your attention enough to read about the life of a bloke you've never heard of, who is still alive and kicking and performing? Intrigued? Then I'll be very happy if you purchase this man's life's work, and sit in Wetherspoon's with a cheap pint and hopefully, enjoy my roller coaster ride of life's ups and downs as a court jester to the adoring public.

Chapter 1

Family Planning

On July 20th 1952, my mother, Joan Burkitt, was in labour. My dad wasn't there because he was conservative. She was in the Townend Maternity Home on Cottingham Road, Hull. She tried to push me into the world with the aid of hot sweaty hands belonging to a midwife poking and prodding my bald head with encouraging words; 'It's nearly there'; 'Keep pushing'; 'Not long now'. I thought, 'Someone's bringing in a wheelbarrow full of cement, maybe it's my mother', because I could hear her grunting and swearing. Was this midwife going to grab me by the head and bury me under concrete, similar to a London gangster hiding a dead body on the M62?

I was contemplating whether to stay where I was and not come out, due to the noise and puffing my mother was making and all that swearing. What language! I knew my father wasn't there as she never called his name once. ('Len, you bastard!') I could only guess I had a father. I was just about to turn round and go back when daylight appeared and those big hands grabbed my cranium and pulled me head first into the face of Nurse Diesel from the Mel Brooks film High Anxiety. Now, I know I was ugly – all babies are – but when I saw her face I screamed. And because I screamed, she smacked my bottom and laid me on my mother's chest between two puppies with red noses. I've been frightened of dogs ever since, especially when my mother tried to get me to eat one. Never again!

I don't remember much after that until I was five, apart from I had a lot of rusks, slept in a pram and saw a lot of the puppies (very close up). They must have been blind because they didn't have any eyes. My mother carried them everywhere and she even had two little pouches strapped to her front, in case they fell out!

Joey Who?

I was the first child and given lots of attention. My father was shown none and retired to his garden, his shed, his tomatoes and chrysanthemums, where he watered his plants and sprayed me with his hosepipe as I sat in my Silver Cross pram doing Frank Spencer impressions in a white knitted beret. (Mmmmm – nice.) Over the years, my granddad came to visit us. He would sit in my dad's shed and take his teeth out to make me laugh. With my father, Granddad and me in the shed, the prefab we lived in was quite empty so my mother took in lodgers to pay the rent. She had two men and a baby to look after and what with steeping Granddad's long johns, boiling nappies, trying to smother me in the pram with too many blankets, selling chrysanthemums, spraying Dad's tomatoes with liquid sheep dung, hanging crisp white sheets on the line 'because it's a nice drying day' and opening tins of corn beef, she was a very busy woman. In 1957 she gave birth to my little sister, Wendy. However did she find the time?

My mother was ten years younger than my father and a very attractive woman. She was one of four sisters and three brothers. She loved family, loved a laugh and loved my sister and me. I think she once loved my father but we never saw this. Her life was a busy, day to day routine at home, and at her part time job as a school cleaner, to save whatever money she could to help pay the bills. She was an excellent manager.

She wanted my father to go far, so he did – he biked to Bridlington on a weekend. My father was a quiet man. He spent most of his life riding his bike to work and watering plants. He was a joiner and made things in the shed. He once threatened to make my mother a coffin if she didn't stop nagging!

My mother wanted him to work for himself and build caravans and bungalows. He built one two bedroomed bungalow in timber on the east coast near Bridlington but it was burnt down by the landlord wanting more ground rent. (They thought it was me, the family arsonist). My father refused to pay. The site is still there; it's called Wilsthorpe

Holiday Park. In those days it was Wilsthorpe Camp. I've been to see where his bungalow was. There's a little plaque in his honour which says 'Firewood – fifty pence a bundle'

My father had a very dry sense of humour. He could sit in company for an hour not say a word and then hit you with a one liner that would make everyone fall about laughing. He would do funny walks in public and frighten my sister. Once, he pretended to be a ghost and ran into our bedroom with a red cross painted in lipstick on his forehead because The News of the World front page had said a man claiming to be Jesus had risen from the dead with a red cross tattooed on his head. My mother threatened to leave him. She was always leaving him.

He'd spent the Second World War as a prisoner of war, captured in Italy and moved to Dresden, Germany. He was a prisoner for five years and never spoke about this time. I would ask him about the war but he was not forthcoming in sharing his experiences, apart from putting barbed wire around our house and building a cooling tower with a spotlight in the garden, where he put me inside for three weeks at a time for trampling on his chrysanthemums and kicking footballs through his greenhouse. That was the closest we got. He would stand my toy German soldiers in the garden rockery on guard to make him feel at home.

Talking of barbed wire, we once had a Peeping Tom. This man had been peeping through people's windows for three weeks. The police hadn't seen him but he'd been spotted by the neighbours. At night we had footprints in the mud on the gardens so a neighbourhood watch vigilante group had been set up. This comprised of neighbours on guard in my father's cooling tower, manning the spotlight and residents in their houses hiding behind curtains to witness if and when he would strike again. The toy soldiers marched up and down outside the prefab.

My father set traps in the garden made of empty bean tins on strings (we lived on beans for a month) so we would hear them rattle as Tom the Peeper hopefully tripped over them in the dark. My father dug holes

15

and covered them with plastic sheeting; he put broken glass and rocks in the hole then covered the sheeting with grass. It was like a minefield out there; nobody would dare walk in the garden!

After three weeks nothing happened. Tom was still at large, peeping through windows then skipping away into the night like a phantom voyeur. He never fell over the tins or in the holes. One night, Wendy and I were in bed and my father was shaving in the bathroom in his underpants, vest and slippers. Mother had rollers in her hair and her quilted pink dressing gown on as she drew the front room curtains before bedtime. We heard her scream as Tom the Peeper was standing outside, looking through the corner of the window. My father nearly cut his throat shaving. He dropped his razor and ran out of the front door, with my mother shouting, 'Len, it's him!' My father then ran down our front path and vaulted over the front gate. He had to hurdle it because it was tied up with string; another deterrent to keep Tom out.

Next door's Alsatian dog started to bark and Maisy our neighbour on hearing the scuffle, put her lights on and let the dog out and he ran alongside my father. This had now turned into a scene from Chariots of Fire. Tom was running for his life, as Len Daley Thomson, together with Rin Tin Tin sprinted down the street, with my mother shouting, 'Len leave him, leave him!'

By now, house lights had started to come on, with other residents coming to their front doors in their pyjamas to witness Len Burkitt chasing Tom the Peeper. One or two joined in and under the yellow street lights the chase looked like a Carry on film or a Brian Rix farce. The road was wet and my father tripped in his slippers and fell to the kerb. Rin Tin Tin stood and looked at my father who now, with one slipper on and one off and a cut knee, shouted Get him boy!' The dog, daft as a brush, stood over my father and licked his face. My father stood up and continued the chase with the dog loving this game and waiting for Dad to throw him a stick!

By now, Tom was getting away but feared this big black Alsatian barking and running alongside the marathon man. My father, with determination and his Olympic training as a hurdler and 100 yards sprinter, together with true grit (stuck in his knee), gained on Tom and Len pulled him to the ground. Tom, cowering on the floor said, 'Don't hit me – wearing glasses,' so my father took them off and smacked him in the face!

Dad picked him up and walked him to a waiting police car. Len was a hero, standing there in his skivvies and vest as he limped home with Maisy's dog by his side. Neighbours patted him on the back and my mother met him with her old dressing gown to cover his string vest and well worn grey muddy underpants and praised him with, 'Cover yourself up!'

My father could never please my mother in all aspects of life. She threw his underpants and vest away, bought him new ones and exhibited the top and bottoms on our washing line so the neighbours could see 'he had more than one pair.' That was Len Burkitt, my dad.

My father was not ambitious but my mother was. She encouraged me with my drumming and came to all my school concerts and open days. She bought me extra little bits for my drum kit on birthdays and Christmas and supported me until she died in her late seventies. She was still looking after my father and providing him with clean underpants and vests when she visited him every day in the care home where he ended his life, aged ninety one.

Chapter 2

Looking for Trouble

After crawling out of the pram and throwing away my beret, I enjoyed toddler life, playing on my three wheeler bike and finding Grandad's false teeth in the garden rockery as he walked around, gurning for the neighbours and next door's ginger tom.

After Grandma died, my mother and father took him into our home (Granddad, not the cat), making us a family of four. We only had two bedrooms in the prefab and with me sleeping standing up in the pram in one bedroom, it got a little congested so my mother, father and granddad shared the other bed! After Wendy was born, we had to move to another house for extra space. The Silver Cross was taking up all the room so the days in the prefab were numbered.

The memories of those long summer days, playing in the open fields with the warmth of the sun on the back of your legs cannot be forgotten. In fact, it was so warm one day I set a field on fire with a Craven A fag nicked out of my mother's handbag. I can see the burnt grass now, smouldering as the Fire Brigade arrived and hosed the field down. It was like a sea of black toast. Not a twig, leaf or blade of grass survived. This seemed to be the start of misfortune which I'm afraid has followed me around for the last sixty five years. I should have written Arthurs Brown's hit song 'Fire' and worn a hat with flames coming out of the top and become a one hit wonder! Trouble always found me and I was very accident prone. I visited Hull Royal Infirmary's A & E department four times before it officially opened.

When I was seven, one day, in a field near our house, a tree fell on my head when it was cut down by a so - called friend as we pretended to be in the U.S.Cavalry. I entered the fort on my imaginary horse through the gates which were the big branches suspended by a rope. As

I stood underneath the gap to ride into the fort to take the salute, my friend cut the rope. The tree fell on my head and he was beside himself with laughter. I limped home on my imaginary horse to my mother, who was not amused, but she put a bandage round the lump, making me look like John Hurt in The Elephant Man.

That same year I fell in Peasholme Park boating lake in Scarborough as I tried to jump across rocks surfacing on top of the water. I was wearing my best two piece suit and had to walk around all day wearing my mother's cardigan with my legs in the arms, buttons up the back and paper towels in my shoes.

But the worst trauma was when I was six. It was a windy November afternoon and nearly dark. I was waiting for my mother to collect me outside Endyke Lane Infant School. She usually arrived at 3.30pm prompt to collect me and to sell tomatoes and chrysanthemums from the Silver Cross pram which now doubled up as a fruit and vegetable barrow. She also sold pegs and made a nice pink carnation from a coat hanger and toilet tissue. At 3.35pm no mother appeared, so being the adventurer that I am, I decided to cross the busy road alone. I took two steps off the kerb and headed towards the middle of the road. A fellow on a motorbike hit me side on, and the chinstrap of my leather helmet caught underneath his handlebars and he dragged me twenty yards down the road. Realizing I wouldn't be paying for the fare, he brushed me aside with his motorcycle gauntlet. I hit the road and he sped off in fright, not even giving me a ticket for the ride.

I was taken by the school's headmistress in her green Ford Pop to the children's hospital. My chinstrap, which was now welded to my lower jaw and looked like a cockeyed bobby's helmet, had to be cut free as it had embedded itself into my jawbone. My jaw and throat looked like a rabbit's neck hanging in a butcher's shop. The Police were contacted and a policeman said, 'I have a helmet that looks just like that.' The event was witnessed by a pedestrian but the hit and run motorcyclist was never found.

However, after a week off school convalescing, still with a bandaged head, a mystery parcel arrived containing – guess what? The other half of my helmet? No. A jumbo pack of Rowntree's wine gums. Well, to chew wine gums was impossible, so I thought, the bastard wanted to hurt me again! The gift was anonymous so a deep feeling of guilt and worry probably hung over the motorcyclist. He obviously daren't go to the Police as this was a hit and run of a child and possibly meant a jail sentence. When my jaw got better and I could chew, I ate the wine gums, never wore another leather helmet and crossed the road on zebra crossings until I was twenty eight. My mother sold fruit and vegetables from the Silver Cross on the zebra crossing and from that day everything was black and white.

I'll extend my medical report and accidents later as we skip through the years into my teens, as I diced with death on several occasions throughout my colourful youth.

Chapter 3

From Tins to Skins

When I was not spending time in A &E, I would sit on the shed roof at the prefab and teach myself the art of drumming. This was achieved by using two kitchen knives played on an empty Mackintosh toffee tin. I became very proficient at military band marches, accompanying the drumming with a one man band effect by using my mouth as a trumpet. When we eventually moved to Bentley Grove on a large housing estate in Hull, this practise continued and developed from knives and a tin to knitting needles and plastic Tupperware containers which I played in our new front room on my improvised drum kit.

It was the early sixties; pop music and The Beatles were becoming more and more popular and the highlight of the week, for me, would be to drum to the music presented on a new Saturday night television pop programme, Thank Your Lucky Stars. As well as The Beatles, I drummed fanatically to The Kinks, The Who, Gerry & the Pacemakers, and many more. My skills developed during this time but my drum kit got less and less because my mother pinched my snare drum and floor tom-tom to put Dad's tomatoes in to keep them fresh.

On my ninth birthday, I begged for proper drums after coming third in a talent competition in the open air theatre in Scarborough. I had to drum with The Ken Ford Band to a rendition of 'The Rise and Fall of Flingle Bunt' by the Shadows and then the finale of 'The William Tell Overture', both of which had drum solos in the middle. I proceeded to knock seven bells out of the resident drummer's kit. Now, this kit was different to my Tupperware boxes and I hit everything in sight! The stool was too high for my small legs dangling in my khaki shorts with white ankle socks inside my Clark's sandals. So with some adjustment to the seat, my right leg found the bass drum pedal, my left leg the hi hat cymbal, similar to a busker slapping his knees together while playing the drums and making the sounds of a trumpet all at once. Well, I was experienced at this – I just had to find a shed to sit on. With sticks flying, I won fifteen shillings. I was beaten by a curly headed six year old blonde girl singing 'On the Good Ship Lollipop' and a blond German boy from the Hitler Youth playing Mozart on the piano. I was the only one on the bill not blond. I think the show was sponsored by Wella Hair Products and that's why I came third!

I was congratulated by the audience as we left to go back to our guest house and as we sat in the tram car travelling up the cliff a lady said to me, 'You're very good. Do you have a little drum kit at home?' to which my mother replied, 'We're going to buy him one for Christmas.' I thought, 'Great – a proper kit'. But she got me a Marks & Spencer Christmas cake tin with some knitted drumsticks so I couldn't be heard! No, she rode her bike to Pools Corner, a second hand shop on Newland Avenue and bought me a snare drum and cymbal for £12. She folded them up and put them in her bicycle basket and peddled home. By now the Silver Cross was used for my sister Wendy. She had to sit at the back under the hood because the front of the pram was full of tomatoes and chrysanthemums! On Christmas morning, there it stood in the front room, a red pearl Olympic snare drum and a six inch cymbal, together with drumsticks and brushes.

Along with selling fruit and vegetables from the pram, Mum was also a school cleaner and worked very hard to give my sister and me little treats. When I was ten she bought me a second hand Alba record player which came with five 45's records. They were 'Picture of You', Joe Brown, 'Bobby's girl', Susan Maughan, 'She Taught me to Yodel', Frank Ifield, 'Let's Dance', Chris Montez, and 'Stranger on the Shore', Acker Bilk. I remember them so vividly because I drummed constantly to these songs for three weeks, day in, day out. The neighbours thought I was building a shed and were pleased I got a paper round after school to relieve the banging. I fooled them because the only reason I got a job was to buy more records and continue the banging as a front room drummer!

With new records bought for a shilling and sixpence, out of my twelve shillings earnings as a paper boy, less five Park Drive fags at a shilling, I could buy five or six new records a week. By then, my snare drum was getting beaten to death as I bashed out four in a bar to The Kinks, The Hollies, The Beatles and The Stones. Sometimes, I heard the neighbours joining in, keeping time as they banged on the wall but this didn't deter me or dampen my enthusiasm. The next Christmas, by surprise, my father bought me a brand new red pearl bass drum from Gough & Davey's music shop in the town. Twenty one pounds this cost – I couldn't believe this goodwill gesture from my father; after all, he hardly ever spoke to me. Only when I kicked footballs through his greenhouse window would he shout, 'Come here you little bastard! 'so I knew he wasn't my real father! I think my mother must have made him go into the shed and peel off four fivers out of the tin he kept in his secret drawer that he thought no-one knew about.

In my early days she gave me money from her savings kept in different socks which were hidden all round the house. There was a sock for gas money, a sock for electric money, a sock for holidays and a wellington boot for a rainy day. I often wondered why my father walked around all day in one sock and paddled in puddles wearing only one boot when it rained.

Neither of my parents earned much money but were excellent managers and never wasted a penny. My sister and I were just the same and together when we were on holiday my mother, father, Wendy and I would sit outside public toilets, all dying to go but wouldn't spend a penny!

We were both encouraged to save and on a Monday morning with my two shillings and sixpence pocket money, before the days of a paper round, I would skip in my shorts and Clark's sandals to the Yorkshire Penny Bank and deposit a shilling and sixpence, leaving a whole shilling to spend on myself. The shilling was used for socialising as I was now in a gang of friends and had to contribute to the fags, sweets and lemonade we shared together in our den.

This was a damp, smelly air raid shelter at the bottom of David Wade's grandma's garden. There was a rabbit hutch in there containing old wet hay. The entrance was covered with a piece of smelly carpet nailed to the wall and we held corporate meetings daily, looking at our stocks and shares and how much I had in the Yorkshire Penny Bank. We sat in old armchairs with the springs missing. It was home from home! Girls were encouraged to enter this den of nicotine as we chain smoked Players No.6 fags and showed off our singing and miming skills to Beatles records on David's record player. When it got dark, we lit candles and John, Paul, George and Ringo who were actually Keith Mullens, Ronnie Brown, David Wade and me, pulled back the carpet from the doorway and scurried along the dimly lit damp streets of North Hull Estate scavenging and foraging like rats in search of booty.

These were found at the local pub. We would wait in the bushes whilst Ronnie Brown, the group 'tea leaf', would nip into the off licence, lift the counter lid and proceed to steal things behind the counter while the barmaid was serving in the bar. He trained in the air raid shelter and we timed him. He could get crisps, a packet of cigs, a Cadbury's dairy milk, and a bottle of pop under his coat and in his pocket in 30 seconds! He would wear his shoplifting coat with large pockets, stuff as much in as possible, and when the barmaid finally came through from the bar to serve him he would buy a penny liquorice (the penny was provided from group subs) and leave. We would then run like the clappers down back alleys and across the fields to feast on this bounty in the clubhouse. We would eat the lot until we felt very sick and it was nearly dark; the candles would burn out and we would walk home smelling of smoke, a damp old settee and straw.

As well as being thieves, the gang was a well organised and highly tuned army commando unit which included a football and cricket team.

We played war, killing each other every day in the long grass of King George V playing fields. We had three day cricket matches with our wickets, bats, pads and caps. We also played five a side football games on the field against the other streets. We had a full strip, all matching in green. Where did the money come from? Yes, you've guessed it – Ronnie Brown! As well as trips out to the pub, he was very good at pinching lemonade and milk money left out on the step by customers for the milkman or lemonade man. In those days, these were all delivered to most houses on a daily basis. Ronnie would knock on the door and if people were out he would take the money from the step. He once called for me at the back door, pinched our lemonade money and then denied it. What a lad! I think he ended up doing the Great Train Robbery with his namesake Ronnie Biggs.

When not spending time through the summer days playing football, cricket and fighting Germans, I was still drumming in the front room. As kids of eleven and twelve we were all obsessed with pop music. We were in the midst of a cultural revolution brought about by the desire for change. The Beatles, the Rolling Stones and anyone else in the top twenty were our inspiration for a different life to the one our parents had grown up with. After the Second World War men came home to their sweethearts and set up house (if you still had a house and not many people did in Hull), they got married and looked for a job. They wanted the security of a peaceful life without war. By 1958 we wanted things to be different.

With the advent of Elvis, Buddy Holly, Little Richard and Jerry Lee Lewis from America, and the Beatles and the Stones and other groups in the UK, they introduced R &B and rock and roll to British kids. No more Kenny Ball's Jazzmen, no more Micki & Griff, no more Max Bygraves etc. Our parents had had listened to music such as this for the last five years on the BBC Light Programme. That was about all there was, but now – beat music! Every spare minute, kids listened to this new sensation on Radio Luxemburg and Radio Caroline; on transistor radios, under the sheets, in the toilet, inside their school desks. Our parents hated it, we loved it. This was a revolution and the music was the beginning of a new culture and society that would and has changed the world.

We embraced it every minute of the day, and pop music, apart from school, took over our lives. I was drumming to it every day after school, while my mother was at work and before my father came in. Don't forget I was still accident prone and was told by my mother not to let the fire go out before my father came in. Considering I had all the Top Twenty to drum through before 5.30pm when Dad would arrive home from work, one afternoon I let the drum sticks fly and forgot about the fire as it dwindled away. Now, I wasn't too old to get a clout from my dad and would do if he saw what had happened.

Endeavouring to save the situation, I'd seen my mother put a little paraffin on the fire in the past to 'cheer it up' if it was dying so I thought I would 'cheer it up'. I went for the Esso Blue tin and let a few drops mix with the now dying embers. A little puff of flame showed its face and then disappeared once again to nothing. I gave it a few more drops, once again a glimmer of hope, then nothing. So I held the can over the embers and let it glug for a couple of seconds. Whoof! The bloody lot went up and the flames shot up the chimney, setting it alight. I ran outside to see black smoke bellowing from the stack and all the kids in the street gawping, thinking the house had been bombed. Inside, the flames were two foot high in the fireplace and soot and smoke were filling the front room. Wendy was playing with her dolls upstairs and I shouted, 'Look what I've done!' This wasn't a boast, it was a panic. Wendy ran downstairs and my mother walked in from work. 'Wait till your father gets home', she said. 'You'd better hide'. She then ran to the telephone directory and in panic looked under F for Fire Brigade instead of just dialling 999. She wasn't in any mood to be advised so Wendy and I ran down the garden and locked ourselves in the garden shed.

The Fire Brigade was alerted and as Wendy and I sat sobbing in the shed we could hear the fire engine bells in the distance. We all go through the same thoughts when a fire engine passes us in the street, don't we? 'I hope it's not my house'. Well, as my father was biking home from work, he would have thought the same. But it was! The fire engine passed Len and he arrived home to see my mother and a crowd of neighbours standing outside our house as firemen entered the premises with large hoses and pumped water up the fireplace and down the chimney.

My dad shot off his bike and started moving the settee and mats out of the front room into the garden along with anything else he could save from water damage. I dared to look through the shed window and I was filling my pants. Wendy was still crying and I couldn't contemplate coming out of this alive. Would this be a good time to leave home? My dad was always telling me to 'Bugger off! '. Could I get out of the shed without being spotted?

Once all the furniture was in the garden, the neighbours had a look round and made offers on the three piece suite, Granddad's old chair, the television and sideboard. Kids were banging on the shed window and laughing, knowing my last rites were only minutes away. Should a priest or vicar be summoned to protect me from my father? Then, it happened. I saw my dad coming towards the shed. Someone shouted, 'You're in for it now – can I have your drums'? Dad banged on the shed door. 'Open this door' he shouted. 'Please don't hit us, Dad,' we said. Wendy was by now hopping on one leg, like little girls do when they want to go to the toilet. 'Open this door,' he shouted again. 'Not if you're going to hit me,' I shouted back. My mother ran down the path. 'Len, don't hit him,' she yelled. The neighbours and kids were loving this. The scenario was similar to Tom the Peeper. We'd heard these words before. But instead of Tom shouting them it was me, his son. Mum said, 'Howard, open that door'! I wished I had been called Joey then, because I would have replied, 'There's no Howard in here.' My mother pushed my father out the way. I opened the door and let Wendy out. She ran to my mother and I slammed it shut again as my father tried to grab me and pull me out through the keyhole!

I stayed in the shed until the fire engine had gone, the neighbours had left and my father had finished cleaning the furniture in the garden. When it was getting dark and the house lights were going on all over the neighbourhood I decided to be brave and leave the shed. Dad was either going to hit me or he'd calmed down. I put the key in the lock to let myself out. It wouldn't turn. He'd locked me in with a spare key and put it in the lock at the other side. This, I thought, would resemble tactics against the Germans as Field Marshal Rommel had tried to enter my father's hut when he was a prisoner of war. He shouted 'Len, ler us in, I'm gonna swop ya sheets.' Rommel pretended he was from Gateshead but my father wouldn't be fooled by this German ploy and not concerned or worried about clean sheets. Instead, he made another key from a bar of soap and kept the Germans locked out until the end of the war. With no clean sheets or soap, the men got fleas and lice and cooked them in a wok. They opened a Chinese takeaway and called it, 'Wok around the clock'!

At about 9pm, after I had been in the shed for over four hours, I heard someone walking down the path. The key turned in the lock and the door opened. A torch shone through the darkness and a plate with a custard cream was pushed in my direction, together with my plastic Indian water bottle and my pyjamas. The door was locked again. He made me sit in the dark for another ten minutes before my mother and Wendy arrived to let me out.

There were rumours in the street my father was going to 'set the shed on fire – see how he likes it', and even one that he'd thrown my drums in as well. (Most neighbours were praying for this to happen) I came out of the shed very sheepish and was sent straight to bed. My dad didn't speak to me for days. This wasn't unusual but I kept out of his way. I was the talk of the estate and school. Jokes appeared like,

'Are you hot under the collar'? and 'Smoke gets in your eyes' and 'Up on the roof' were sung to me at school.

I'll always remember that night, lying in bed, pulling back the sheets, looking at the moon through the window and thinking, 'Don't ever use paraffin to make a fire, rub two drum sticks together – that'll do.'

Chapter 4

Drumming up a Storm

School didn't hold a great significance in my life. I got dressed and went every morning. I liked art, technical drawing and history and enjoyed football and the school plays but I couldn't wait for home time to play the drums until Dad came home. Then I would play out until it was dark with the thieves and vagabonds that graced our neighbourhood.

One night on the playing fields we spotted a well organised soccer team of 'posh' lads. They were from the local Baptist church and part of the Boys Brigade. It was like the scouts but without shorts. They were famous for their marching bands of drummers, buglers and trumpeters. I'd seen them many times in the town on parades.

Well, these lads could play football as well and they asked if Barry and Robert Dixon and I wanted to join in. At the time, we didn't realise this was a recruitment plot! We put on our soccer boots and from that evening I became a member of the Boys Brigade for the next eight years.

In the 1960's boys' clubs were popular. The scouts, sea cadets and air training corps all flourished. I think the Government was getting us all trained for another war. Boys at that time loved war. At school that's what we played, that and cowboys and Indians. We were obsessed with battles, tanks, guns and Wild West films. Every boy imagined himself as John Wayne with a green beret (I had a white one), Wyatt Earp or the sheriff from Dodge City. We all carried pretend guns and spat out imaginary bullets all day long. My school jumper was covered in spit from every other kid who spat from his imaginary tommy gun.

But when we joined the BB, this was kind of real. We had uniforms consisting of a black pill box hat with two white stripes. This had to be

Blancoed (that is, whitened with runny white paint). Also, a white shirt pressed and ironed, a school blazer, black tie and white haversack which had to be starched, with brass buttons to be polished. We polished and shone our brown leather belts with boot polish. We also pinned on medals and awards we received for bravery, fighting the rough kids on the estate who took the piss.

We became very competitive and proud and fought for the best drill squads, the best PT team, and the best soccer team in the battalion. There were battalions all over the country and we travelled as far away as London and Bradford to compete against other boys.

We participated in great battalion camps on the Isle of Wight. A removal lorry would leave our church on the Friday, complete with tents, tables, chairs, pots and pans etc and forty boys with suitcases. We would arrive in the IOW via the ferry from Portsmouth eight hours later. We'd then set up camp for a week of outdoor activities and mischief. Battalions were from all over the country and the rivalry between different companies was rife. We loved attacking each different camp in the middle of the night, nicking their flags off their flag poles and hoisting them up in our camp.

One night, we did a raid in the dark at a strange camp, looking for their tuck. Every camp had a tuck tent full of crisps, lemonade and sweets. There were boxes of these, enough for forty boys for a week. The shop was open twice a day and you bought what you liked. Now, Ronnie Brown was not in the Boys Brigade so I had to put my skills into action. I carefully took hold of one of the tent flaps to pull back the canvas, put my hand in and have a feel around. But instead of tuck, I had my hand on what turned out to be a human being. There was a terrific scream as I fondled the chest of a female! You have never seen six boys on a commando mission run so fast in the dark, through cow shit, nettles, brambles and thistles, to save their lives. Apart from our torches it was pitch black. We had planned the raid to the exact detail. No moon, steal their tuck and their flag and get away. But it was so dark

31

we had wandered into the wrong camp. A camp full of Girl Guides! It was the first touch I had ever had of the female form.

To make matters worse, when we sneaked back to our camp, the other boys in our battalion had emptied our tent, strewn our suitcases on the grass, emptied the contents and thrown all our clothes and sleeping bags on top of the main marquee. We sat all night in our tent, waiting for dawn, until we could retrieve our belongings. We stood on each other's shoulders with a yard brush, knocking the clothes to the ground and whispering, 'That's yours', 'Is that mine?' 'No, whose are these?' It was like the first day of a Primark sale as we stood in a wet field sorting out shirts, underpants, socks, pyjamas and vests. I could just imagine the other boys in the tents with their hands over their mouths, pissing themselves with laughter as if we were having an early morning jumble sale.

All the things we got up to, all the mischief, was not in keeping with the Baptist church. Punishments were dished out and privileges were withdrawn at home and abroad when we were caught doing what young boys do.

We all competed for the Duke of Edinburgh's Award. There were three medals; bronze, silver and gold, in sport, swimming, rock climbing, sailing, canoeing, first aid and camping. In fact, everything to give young people the opportunity to achieve personal goals in outdoor pursuits. I had done my first aid, swimming, camping and walking. I only had the canoeing to pass to get my bronze. The silver and gold were hard to achieve and the gold would usually take around three years to pass and would be presented at Buckingham Palace by the Duke himself.

Twelve boys from our battalion set off for Ripon in the North Yorkshire Dales and after setting up camp, hit the river and had the first lessons in canoeing. The current was fast and we were guided into the water and shown how to survive if the canoe capsized. The Eskimo roll is the drill used as you throw your paddle to the shore, bend your head forward, grip the sides of the canoe, lean to the left and submerge yourself under the water. The watertight apron stretched around your body will keep the water out as you roll underneath the canoe and pull yourself up and back to the surface.

This is a frightening experience at the best of times, just waiting for a novice canoeist to have an accident. Well, in my case it didn't have to wait long. As I threw my paddle to the shore, I took a deep breath and rolled the canoe upside down. My apron came adrift and the canoe filled with water. Now, if you can imagine being in the bath and somebody throws in a Labrador and it splashes everywhere in sight and pulls you under – well, that's what it was like. As I gasped, my mouth opened and I got a gob full of water. Kicking and struggling with my apron around my legs, coughing and trying to breath at the same time, to surface is not an easy feat. My legs were still part of the canoe as the current took me further down the river. Then, an instructor came after me in his canoe and grabbed the front of mine, with me upside down in the bottom. I couldn't see him but felt this sudden charge of movement and imagined a shark or whale was now taking me to the depths of the river and I would never be seen again.

Within seconds (which is a lifetime when you are drowning) I felt hands around my neck from behind my head. I thought, 'This whale is now trying to strangle me.' Then it spoke. 'Don't panic, stop struggling, relax – I've got you!'. A speaking whale – what a novelty! Where was it taking me? Any minute, I expected my head to leave my body as Jaws 3J was being filmed on the banks of the River Snell. I was rescued by the instructor and swimming against the current, he got me to the bank and I was dragged out of the river like a wet cloth.

As you would expect I didn't attempt my Eskimo roll again that weekend and didn't achieve my bronze medal. Not deterred by my adventure, I was encouraged to try again later in the year and headed off to Fraisthorpe on the North East coast and tried again in the North Sea. This time it was summer and holiday makers were on the beach and it was a nice calm summer's day. I set off, once again determined to do what Eskimos do when they want a roll, and paddled into the wild blue yonder. My accomplice was in another canoe, paddling behind me. He had to verify I'd complete the roll successfully and log it in his book of achievements. If you are familiar with the sea near this coast, the water is usually a cloudy blue which changes to green and finally, around half a mile out it changes to dark blue. Well, paddling away, enjoying myself, I ventured out unknowingly into the deep blue and could see the people on the beach who now resembled matchstick men. The waves were getting bigger and crashing onto the front of the canoe. Not realising how far out I was, my pal in the other canoe was waving for me to come further into shore. I waved back, thinking he was missing me. A large wave hit the front and the canoe upturned.

With not an Eskimo in sight, I went under and hung onto the upturned hull. Taking out my sodden emergency manual, I remembered you had to swim to the end of the hull, take hold of the lanyard (that's the rope around the cockpit) and swim to the shore, pulling your canoe behind you. Considering I had only passed my 3rd class swimming certificate in the public baths doing six lengths, this was a different ball game. I was wearing a kagoul, jeans, jumper and plimsolls and the waves were smacking into my face. I was now drifting towards Rotterdam! My companion had seen what had happened so he turned his canoe in my direction and made waves towards me.

In the meantime, a man on the beach, a canoe voyeur with binoculars, spotted my predicament. He threw his clothes on the beach and swam out towards me. Now this guy could move, and the race was on. Who would reach me first, Davy Crockett or Duncan Goodhew?

Holding the canoe for buoyancy, I hung on and tried to swim on my back towards the shore, gulping great amounts of salt water by the minute. This makes you cough and out of breath. I had lost the paddle and could only wish that rescue was on the way. The beach swimmer, complete with outboard motor strapped to his Speedos, got to me first. I think he could have swum the channel with the strength in his arms and body. Once again I heard the familiar words, 'I've got you, don't struggle, leave go of the canoe.' He put his arms round my waist and started to swim towards the shore. My pal in his canoe arrived five minutes later after going for an ice cream and waving to the people on the beach, who now were watching with great interest. He grabbed the lanyard around the canoe and towed it back to shore with my saviour and me hanging on the back, dog paddling.

We arrived around twenty minutes later to a hero's welcome; the swimmer was patted on the back and congratulated as I lay on the sand totally exhausted. Once again I had crossed the boundaries of uncertainty. I had ventured to the depths of the unknown and hung on to the precipice of danger. What a wanker!

I decided that water sports were not for me although being a Cancerian, I loved the stuff. I eventually achieved my Duke of Edinburgh Bronze award, passing in bird watching, flower arranging and train spotting!

Chapter 5

Marching to Pop

Now, you might say to me, 'What about the drumming?' Well, as the water sports took a back seat I was now promoting my talents in the Boys Brigade band. I'd forgiven the older boys who had emptied my tent at the Isle of Wight, and they'd asked me to play drums in their newly founded pop group. They were around sixteen/seventeen years of age and I was twelve.I was still a small child, not a midget but Jimmy Krankie and I had a lot in common; in fact, I looked a lot like him, hence no girls in my life, apart from the odd touch inside a tent once a year.

The group would rehearse after all our other weekly activities and an audience of boys would gather around us like male groupies, drinking coke, eating crisps and dancing with each other. We attempted the hits of the day on two guitars and one microphone, all playing through an eighteen inch speaker and a thirty watt amplifier. We sounded shit, we were shit but nobody else knew! We had no competition as there was no one to compare us with, so when the girl guides had a dance, guess who was booked to play? They loved us and 'Take That' was born!

As well as pop music, boys who could play an instrument were enlisted and trained for the City band. This was made of budding bugle players, trumpeters, drummers and xylophone players who could also play in a marching band. You learned the tunes then walked in line, playing your instrument, hopefully not to march into the person in front who could be carrying a bass drum or tuba. If this happened the band went into complete confusion and music and drumsticks were dropped all over the road.

Thirty two of us were in the band and once a month we would parade on a Sunday morning on a church parade. We would leave the cenotaph in Hull city centre at 7.00 am and march down the back streets of Hull. People would rise out of their beds, put on their dressing gowns and slippers, walk to the windows, open their curtains, lift the sash and shout, 'Fuck off!' 'We've only been in bed an hour!' You noisy bastards – go to somebody else's street!' Tin cans and milk bottles would then be aimed, as missiles as buglers and drummers tried to dodge the rapid fire. The bass drummer would shelter behind his bass drum as beer bottles cascaded and ricocheted off the glockenspiels now forming a wall at the back. This happened every month and we were pleased to reassemble to fight another day. One Sunday we were playing Glen Miller's 'Little Brown Jug ' and someone threw one at us! For safety, I decided to stick with the pop group and play indoors at church fetes to swooning Brownies.

When you're young and everyone around you is young, you're flavour of the month for only a certain length of time. It's like the new Christmas puppy; after a while nobody wants to take it for a walk anymore. After six months the group novelty had worn off. We were never going to be the new sensation of Hull – more like four sad lads from Cottingham Road Baptist Church trying to impress the under sixteen's church congregation. I realised there was proper music out there and also a different female species apart from Girl Guides when I was taken to a school youth club on Appleton Road. Every Thursday night two hundred kids would meet in the school hall and dance to a proper disc jockey playing Midtown soul rhythm and blues. Local pop groups would visit weekly and lads from the school were rehearsing a band. I heard them in a class room; the bass guitar thumped through my chest as I walked down the corridor. They were playing The Small Faces and The Who covers, 'Can't Explain' and 'Substitute'. They sounded fantastic and I was smitten! Each guitarist had his own amplifier and speaker, the singer had a pa system and the drummer a full drum kit with mixed cymbals, a mat on the floor and spurs to hold his kit down because he was playing so heavy his kit would move. He also had a chain round his seat to the bass drum's legs to hold the kit in place. This was heavy shit! This was schoolboys being 'pro'. It made our church group sound like The New Seekers. The guitarist was playing solos, not just chords and the singer was a mixture of Mick Jagger and Roger Daltry. I went to watch them practise every week and became a groupie.

Apart from their rehearsals every two weeks, the youth club had a dance featuring visiting pop groups, groups who played all over the county, groups with a van! Groups who played in pubs, dance halls, clubs and in those early days of the sixties, all night festivals. Mick Ronson played with The Rats, a local Hull group who later became David Bowie's Spiders and Robert Palmer fronted The Mandrake from Scarborough and later became a world star. I was lucky to see these perform at our youth club for a fee of £25 for the group. I watched the drummers in every group and at the age of thirteen decided my destiny had been planned. So twiddling my drum sticks, I went to play with Wilf Taylor, a blind organist who performed on the mighty Wurlitzer at the Good Fellowship pub on Cottingham Road. His blind dog lay under the organ as Wilf played every swing classic from the fifties and sixties. Now, this was not exactly 'Ground Control to Major Tom' or 'Satisfaction' but I was playing for lemonade and crisps and learning the rudiments of swing and dance band music.

After about four gigs, it was reported in the paper that Wilf Taylor had been knocked down on a zebra crossing in the town and sadly, died. I think he thought the crossing was a large keyboard and he was trying to play the black and white notes. His dog had led poor Wilf onto the crossing as a car approached and hit him. The dog wasn't injured but maybe he couldn't stand another night lying under the organ listening to 'Begin the Beguine' one more time! Seriously, Wilf was an excellent musician and organist of his day and he died tragically.

I had to move on and my time was spent less at the church and Boys Brigade. I still enjoyed playing in the battalion marching band and enjoyed the competitions and weeks away but realised pop music was inside me and I wanted to make music. I answered adverts in the local paper, scribbled down telephone numbers on cards looking for drummers in the local music shops and for the next five years, learned my trade.

Chapter 6

The Office Boy

I had failed my eleven plus so I went to the Secondary Modern and I stayed there for those five years waiting to leave. School was something you had to attend until 4pm. and after four you could start drumming or playing football or seeing girls.

I saw a lot of girls walking about, girls in school, girls in the playground, girls on the field. I thought girls were nice but until I was fifteen they might have well come from another planet. I was still a small boy; 4 ft 6ins and weighed 6 stone four. I could make the girls laugh but they always seemed to meet the bigger boys and go behind the bike sheds with them. I often took my three wheeler bike with the basket on the front and blocks on the pedals to the sheds and sat waiting for a date but nobody ever came.

In 1968 I left school on the Friday and started work on the Monday. Everybody had a job to go to in those days; hardly any kids were out of work and employment was plentiful. I started on £4.60 a week as an office boy at John Good Shipping Agents in the middle of Hull town centre. I swopped my three wheeler bike for a two wheeler and in my new sports jacket and trousers complete with shirt and tie and Mum's sandwiches, met the rest of the staff who I would work with for the next six months.

Hull in the 1960s was a very busy port of fishing and cargo. The docks were nonstop, with ships transporting goods all around the world as well as importing and distributing them by road and rail to all corners and major cities of the UK.

My job, together with five other office boys, was to sort out mail that came from all over the world, in a large internal sorting office and take it by hand to the different departments on all floors. When this was done we then, with briefcases on bikes, pedalled all around the city of Hull and delivered mail and parcels to other shipping agents, solicitors offices and ships chandlers in the Old Town. I loved the history of the Old Town. The smell of the old offices, climbing the stairs, the old cage lifts and long office corridors full of rooms, and clerks who had been there since the 1940s. Files and papers, dust and dirt filled these offices; many things were still written by hand and on old typewriters that would sit on every desk. It was the first of several jobs I had and I was always sacked due to daydreaming and lack of diligence. I was never suited to working for somebody else but it took me about five jobs before I realised this.

After three weeks at John Good's I was told to put around five hundred letters at 3/- each (15p today)through the franking machine. At 5.30 pm the post van would collect all our post. We had five floors with around three/four departments, all for different countries of the world. Now, this was a lot of post. Most days we would have maybe five/six sacks of letters and parcels to deal with. On this particular day I thought the franking machine was set at 3/- but in fact, it was set at £3. Instead of the cost for post totalling £75 it was £1,500!

I was goose stepped into the office and told that, earning £4.60 per week I would be working for the next seven years free! The alternative was to be sent to New Guinea on a prison ship like Papillon and spend my time in the swamps eating beetles and cockroaches. After great consideration from the Head of Department it was decided I wouldn't be allowed to use the franking machine ever again and my duty from then on would be to collect the sacks from all floors and the other office boys would frank the letters and parcels upon my delivery.

These sacks were heavy and if the lift was busy I had a sweat on, climbing the stairs from different departments, one sack on my back, one under my arm and dragging the rest across the floor. (Now I knew how Father Christmas felt). Apart from this, the word had spread through the company about what I had done and my nickname became

Frank!

I was still playing the drums on a night in pubs and clubs and that gave me another five or six pounds a week. Together, with two jobs, I was earning about £10 a week and I was still only sixteen. My father was only earning £12 as a joiner. I offered him drumming lessons so he could earn more money and have two jobs a week like me. His reply was, 'The only beating of skins I'll do is on your backside' so I beat a hasty retreat!

After spending one Saturday afternoon gazing at drum kits in a local music shop, Gough and Davy (commonly known as Cough and Gravy), I spied an advert on their notice board for a drummer. 'DRUMMER REQUIRED FOR BLUES AND ROCK GROUP'. Was this what I was looking for? I needed a new challenge as I was sick of the pubs and clubs by this point and also accompanying backing singers who thought they were the next Frank Sinatra or Tony Christie so I applied. The name of the band was 'The Clockwork Chicken' which sounded like a windup battery hen!

It was my first experience of playing rock and blues with other musicians, (apart from my mates in the Boys Brigade). Well, I call them 'musicians'; the singer worked as a Hull Parks gardener, the lead guitarist was Denny, a boy from Liverpool who worked in a TV repair shop and Colin, the bass guitarist, was a farm labourer. Colin was even smaller than me and when he stood next to his guitar it was six inches bigger than him. He had hair down to his knees which touched the top of his mud-spattered wellies. He looked like he'd just spent three days in a tent in Glastonbury without a hairbrush. He lived with his mother in a farm labourer's cottage in Ellerker, a village on the outskirts of Hull. That's where we rehearsed – in Colin's shed. I was pleased we spent most of the time there because his shed was cleaner than the cottage. If you can imagine Noah's Ark when they led the animals in two by two, well, this was Colin's living room. There was a wooden trestle table with a breadboard and a milk bottle stuck in the centre of it where a butter dish and bread knife were being bombed by flies. The occasional goat, pig, sheep, dog or chicken would wander in and eat off this table. Colin's mum would offer us a bluebottle sandwich which she had cut off the mouldy loaf which had seen better days at the Last Supper. They were all the most friendly, down to earth country folk you could wish to meet. It's just a pity they'd never seen a flannel, soap or hot water. I'm sure the animals slept on the settee when it rained. We wiped our feet to come out and itched all the way home on the bus.

I would leave work in the town at five o'clock, bike home for 5.45pm and eat the potted meat sandwiches my mother had left me, in ten seconds flat. I did this balanced on one leg whilst changing from my sports jacket and trousers into my trendy hipsters and tee shirt. Then I'd run onto Cottingham Road and catch the 6.15pm bus for Melton, South Cave and Ellerker and finally, Colin's homestead. Our equipment was set up in the shed and after brushing away the pigeon droppings and straw off my drum kit we would work out which pop and rock tunes to play.

After a year's rehearsals, we performed our first gig at North Cave Village Hall to a half empty room of school kids drinking homemade lemonade and skipping around the maypole to Led Zeppelin's 'Stairway to Heaven' – played very badly, I might add. However, Denny was excellent and went on to bigger things and repairing bigger televisions. Our singer sang in tune but should have stuck to singing to his flowers in the park where he could have sung to a bunch of 'em! Colin was a lovely lad but apart from his long hair and wild image, would have been better off in The Archers discussing muck spreading and driving a tractor because that's what he did best!

After many more rehearsals and milking cows, shearing sheep and collecting duck eggs we came to the conclusion that the band was going nowhere, apart from a day out at Newport Agricultural Show and possibly an appearance on Country File. Disillusioned and very frustrated at the lack of progress over the past twelve months, no gigs and no money, I retreated back into the clubs and pubs of Hull once more to earn my £2 a night and accompany every Tom, Dick and Harry who thought they were to become the stars of tomorrow.

The final straw came at John Good's whilst making my post deliveries around the town one day. I had to take documents to Hull Ship Stores on the side of the River Hull. This building had been there over a hundred years and once again, I had many stairs to climb to the reception. It was a very windy day and I leaned my bicycle against a post on the quayside. I took the documents required out of my briefcase and put it underneath the spring carrier on the back of the bike. I trotted into the building with the letters in my hand and the North Sea wind full force in my face. When I came out of the building the bike was nowhere to be seen. I looked in the river and saw the briefcase floating down the River Hull! The bike had blown into the river and drowned, but the briefcase had come to the surface. My jaw dropped and I walked along the quayside trying to persuade the briefcase to come to the quay. Now, the River Hull is about sixty feet wide and the current was taking it merrily into the estuary and eventually, out into the North Sea. As I passed people on the quayside I shouted, 'That's my briefcase – I've lost it!' I gained a lot of sympathy from the onlookers who were enjoying this bit of excitement in their normally boring lunch break. Then taking a turn for the worst, with the letters inside getting heavy and the leather of the case getting wetter, it sank! I had lost the bike and a day's correspondence of important documents in five minutes.

This was going to be hard to tell back at John Good's and after having been given a second chance as Frank, this was not acceptable. Going before the Head of Department again I was told my services were no longer required and like an early Frank Spencer I was considered a liability. I blame it on that white beret my mother had made me wear in the pram. I think it jinxed me for the next few years.

My next encounter with a normal day job was at Henry Booth's, the printers, once again in the office. I got that job because of a girl I knew whose father was the office manager and looking for a junior assistant in the production department. I knew her dad quite well because we would go to her house and play records. I charmed him with my dynamic personality and wit and made his wife laugh. Not asking for references from John Good's which was a surprise, he took me on face value and I started work in my second job.

Henry Booth's made roll tickets for events and theatres, bingo cards and self adhesive labels. Once again, these were sent all over the world. I didn't have to post them, but process them from customers' orders to production work sheets for the factory. We had around twenty office staff and about a hundred people working in the printing factory. Most of the factory staff was made up of women aged from fifteen to sixty five. These girls ran the machines and were supervised by printing engineers who maintained the presses. Two or three times a day I had to walk into the factory to progress chase orders. I was still 4 ft six and 6 stone four and still small for a boy of sixteen. I would take a deep breath and open the factory door, taking my life into my own hands as I was wolf whistled at and verbally abused by women shouting obscenities at this poor little lad. On my birthday, I was man handled by two women who resembled female wrestlers as they removed my trousers and put me upside down in a large waste paper skip. My pants were passed down the factory and hidden while I climbed out of the skip and walked the full length of the machine shops in my underpants, socks and shoes. They did it to everyone; new apprentices, brides-to-be, leaving parties, birthdays – any excuse to have a laugh. In those days it was termed as innocent fun; nowadays it would be gross sexual harassment!

My life was made hell going into that factory until one day I was told a young lady on a machine fancied me I dared to look at her and smiled at her every time I walked past. She was very attractive, smaller than me, wore full make up and had red/ginger spiky hair. She was a mod. Mod girls rode on the back of boys' scooters and wore large green furry parkas and wide denim jeans. Their jeans were turned up to show off their highly polished Doc Martin boots.

Now, I wore a beige British Home Stores jumper, grey trousers, shirt and tie and a blue jacket and I came to work on a pushbike 'Why would she fancy me?' I wondered. In fact, describing that, I was going to work in something that resembled my Boys Brigade uniform! Well, it wasn't far from it. After a couple of weeks grinning at her and having my leg pulled by all and sundry on the factory floor I was persuaded by pressing reports and secret notes she would like to go out with me! Yes, me – an outcast from mainstream society, a small drummer boy in the Boys Brigade for the last eight years, a little chap who played in social clubs and beat the shit out of drum kits. Well, in for a penny, in for a pound. Mike Humphrey, another Boys Brigade lad, and I went babysitting to his sister's house on a Saturday night and one night we took Kathy the mod and her friend there. We kissed on the settee and Kathy became my first proper girlfriend. She loved music and came to all the pubs and clubs I played in. I finished with the Boys Brigade after making a decision Kathy was more fun than marching, plus the fact I had started to grow out of my uniform. Work was not so bad and the humiliation had stopped in the factory as people knew we were going out together.

During that time, I played for 'Genies Lamp', a cabaret club band and later, as resident drummer at different working men's club venues in and around Hull. I played with backing bands and organists to accompany visiting cabaret and club acts, to enhance their performances and make them sound great! Most were very average and a large percentage of them were a poor standard. Most were semi professional, had days jobs and performed on an evening for extra money. When the professional acts came there was a distinctive difference. They could fill a club, had a proper act and good musical arrangements we enjoyed playing. There were acts who thought they were going to be stars and some with heads and egos you couldn't get through the dressing room door.

One night I was playing at the BP Sports and Social Club with an excellent band, the Milner Marshal Quartet. They were very swing and jazz influenced and hated backing the visiting cabaret's 'pop shit' acts. A cocky singer came to the club and presented the band with music which was beautifully presented in leather folders and gold embossed covers. He gave us each a copy and we stood in a line; the piano player, the sax player, the bass player and me. This singer thought he was the dog's bollocks and the band didn't like him. If an act's music was badly written or pop rubbish, as these jazz musicians termed it, they would give them a hard time. It was childish but they regarded it as good fun.

Well, that evening I was also to blame, because the singer stood there and said, 'Open the book and turn to page one'. After fifteen seconds of silence, looking at this manuscript work of art I said, 'I'll start with a prawn cocktail.' The whole band fell about laughing. Frank, the piano player was crying and Dave, the bass player, shut the music and walked out of the room, beside himself! They still tell that tale now and laugh about the moments we shared and the satirical attitude they had towards visiting artists.

Frank, the leader of the band, hated visiting pop groups and would unplug their equipment, play the piano in the wrong key and do anything to make them sound bad. He didn't like me or the compere of the club messing about either. He was a true, old fashioned musician who had played with big bands throughout the forties and fifties and didn't take kindly to a little fun or comedy which Michael the singer and I brought to the bandstand. The audience loved our music but also enjoyed the occasion when Michael pulled me off the drums with a large hook from behind the curtain. I would make him laugh as he called the bingo by playing The Last Post on a harmonica at the side of the stage.

The audience loved the comedy and the gift of making people laugh would eventually lead to a different career for me later in my life. But right then I wanted bigger things in my life. I wanted to play in the top groups so I answered a newspaper ad that read DRUMMER WANTED FOR WORLD CLASS SHOWGROUP.

Two weeks later I met the band leader of this world class show group off the Humber Ferry into Hull. His name was John Bell. He wore a red fez, chocolate coloured full length trench coat and handmade leather boots with elastic sides. I was intrigued by him and his stories of playing all around the world. We laughed and his personality just shone through, along with his outrageous clothes and his love of life. He offered me the job without even hearing me play and within the next three weeks I had quit Henry Booth's and was rehearsing for my debut as a professional drummer with a professional showband. This gig meant I would be away from England, touring for the next eight months. Kathy was upset but very supportive and I explained that if I still loved her when I returned I would marry her. I said I would write to her every week and I did. The year was 1970. I was eighteen. What did I know?

Chapter 7

The Losers

The band was called THE LOSERS and they had been together for over the last ten years, playing all around the world to American servicemen: Army, Navy and Air Force at bases and army instillations where President Nixon had all three services ready and positioned in case of conflicts during the Cold War. They were very successful as an English pop band and cabaret act.

The three original members of the band had been together for three years. A new guitarist had been brought in and the line up was completed. The band now consisted of three boys and two girls. John Bell on rhythm guitar, key boards and vocals; Richard Gabbitas on lead guitar and vocals; Lesley Neilson on bass guitar and vocals, Norma Grant, lead female singer and me on drums and vocals. (Yes – I was singing as well!) In the show biz world of the late sixties and early seventies we had English pop groups making hit singles every month and filling the charts with pop music. We had blues, soul, jazz and Motown – nearly all American export music, which was supplying the Western world with exciting new stuff from Santana to Jimmy Hendrix to The Doors. We also had the variety and cabaret circuits of musicians and acts which I was going to be part of, playing everything from country and western to James Brown and Sly and the Family Stone. We had to learn lots of American pop music to entertain the GI's going to Vietnam. They were the National conscripts to fight the Viet Cong. The soldiers, airmen and sailors were boys from the age of seventeen upwards who would serve six months in Vietnam then return home. They did basic training in the US and after six weeks training in Europe they were sent to Vietnam or stayed in Europe on an Army/Air/Navy base red alert.

49

Joey Who?

From Frankfurt to Berlin, Madrid to Barcelona, from Holland to Belgium, American and British military bases were stationed in Europe. On every base there were supermarkets, restaurants, hypermarkets selling many American goods from fridges to American cars. There were schools, bowling alleys and cabaret/restaurants seating as many as five hundred people to entertain the American soldiers and families away from home.

I had to learn the act and new songs for The Losers and we rehearsed in Hull for three weeks at a working men's club near the docks before we went over to the Continent. I was eighteen and Richard, the new guitar player, a lad from Lincoln, was twenty. He had my sense of humour and we instinctively became the best of pals. The two girls in the band paired up with each other and John Bell, the band leader did his own thing. We had new suits and costumes and a red transit van full of equipment and luggage for the next twelve months. I said goodbye to a very sad Kathy as we embarked on the ferry to Rotterdam, across the North Sea on an adventure of a lifetime which I would never forget.

Our first destination was to Frankfurt. The journey from Hull across the North Sea to Rotterdam can be very rough and it was! John Bell and the girls were experienced travellers and sailors and didn't think anything of the force nine gale. Richard drank himself to sleep. I sat on deck the whole trip, wrapped in a large blanket for the best part of twelve hours, watching the enormous twenty foot waves crashing over the bow of the ship as she cut through the sea. Occasionally, one of the band would come and have a look at me in between their duty free drinking sessions and reassure me I would feel better 'once I got it up'. Seated on deck with my blanket around my head and a sick bag around my neck I didn't want to 'get it up', I just wanted to die and could not stomach the brandy which was shoved under my nose to 'make me feel better'. I sat all night on deck in the dark on my own, listening to the other odd, weary, lonesome travellers shouting 'Hughie' in the distance.

When daylight started to appear I had slept for maybe an hour and the sickness had left me. Lying in my blanket I looked like Old Mother Riley in her shawl as I made my way inside to the cabin. Richard was snoring; he could sleep for Britain, as I found out during the next year.

I got up at 5 am, the ship docked at 6 am and the restaurant was open. I was now hungry. Inside the restaurant I found aluminium dishes of bacon, eggs, beans and sausages in mounds, all waiting to be eaten. There were no passengers. I was the only one in line. The journey had been so bad that no one could face breakfast. The chefs behind the counters gave me a nice round of applause as I threw away my sick bag and indulged myself in an enormous full English plus toast, fried bread and a gallon of hot steaming tea. They were proud of me. I would be proud of myself if I could 'keep it down'. Gradually, one or two brave foreign lorry drivers started to emerge and sample the croissants and coffee, cheeses and cooked meats. 'What kind of a breakfast is that?' I asked myself as I threw up my full English over the side of the ship. Now I felt better! I sat with a glass of water as the rest of the band joined me and ate everything in sight as I ran back and forwards to the john (American for toilet). See – I was becoming American already and I hadn't even met one yet. Although, it wouldn't be long before we were surrounded by them.

The journey through Holland was a first for Richard and me on the motorways alongside waterways, seeing windmills and old ladies in their Dutch caps. I thought, 'What a funny place to wear a contraceptive – on your head!' Most of them looked too old for sex anyway. Dutchmen use clogs for a contraceptive so they can hear themselves coming!

We travelled up the mountains to a beautiful snow resort called Trier. There was a Dutch nightclub there called The Wilhelmshoc. We had been booked to perform there for one night on our way to Frankfurt. It was a regular stop off for English bands and the Dutch audience were very appreciative, especially a Dutch waitress who succumbed to Richard's charm and provided the band with free drinks and Richard, her double bed.

He was very cocky with himself in the morning. Only the second night from home and he'd filled his boots already. John Bell tried to rise to the occasion and make it a 'double Dutch' but got 'blown out' instead. Well, we agreed that was better than nothing. I must point out that this kind of night time activity happened on a regular basis and I was shifted out from bedroom to bedroom on many occasions while this band of wandering minstrels, including the girls, found members of the opposite sex to share a flea-ridden pit with!

I might have been eighteen but I still only looked twelve. I weighed in at about eight stone and stood in my underpants and socks at 5' 4". I was virtually invisible to the opposite sex and just got a pat on the head and a sweet now and again. Richard was around 5'8', very handsome and quite stocky. He charmed the hot pants off women and they loved it. John Bell was also single and after ten years on the road would 'shag a warm scarf'! Women loved his humour, his good fun and his eccentricity and he loved them all.

After travelling for three days we arrived in Frankfurt at The Munchen Hof guest house. This was where the band always stayed and we were greeted as long lost friends. German guest houses are fabulous places, serving the best home cooked food on wooden tables covered in beautiful lace tablecloths. Everything is clean and tidy and German beer and lager is the best in the world. Richard and I shared a room, as did the girls unless they were staying with friends or GIs elsewhere. John Bell had his own room. We were all pleased about that because apart from having nice clothes he was the most untidy scruffy bastard you could meet. When he arrived he would throw his suitcase on the floor and that would be where it stayed, exposing all his dirty washing until we moved to the next gig. Things would crawl out of his suitcase and wash bag and die! This was to be our base for the next few weeks and we would travel on one night stands to different American bases, do our show and travel back.

The first show was a cabaret on a base called Rhein-main Airbase. This was a military airport used only for flying in servicemen and freight from the States. When we arrived there we found it was an enormous airport with flights coming in all the time to and from America and Vietnam. We travelled to the club on the base and this venue was like Batley Variety Club. BVC could seat around two thousand people with two tier seating. At Rhein-main there were cabaret tables lit with table lamps and decorated in red or gold with furniture to match. The stage would be a large pull out on top of a vast dance floor with stage and theatre lighting. This was my first glimpse of a swank night club. This and many more clubs on bases throughout Europe were the same, as I would experience in the months to come. They played host to top American stars who flew from the States to entertain the troops abroad. Our first night was no exception and The Losers were to support The Everly Brothers! This was an enormous surprise and a shock to our confidence. We were told everything would be fine and we would open the show. Now, for a little drummer boy from Hull who looked like his mother had just left him at the shops, I felt a bit out of my depth as I stood and watched the Everly Brothers' equipment being brought onto the stage. This was professional gear. They hadn't travelled three days in a transit van with a bass drum on their legs and a guitar case around their necks. They had roadies – people to set up the stuff. A Ludwig drum kit (at that time one of the best kits in the world), came in with Paiste cymbals and stands. The drum stool on their kit would have cost more than all my drums together.

I was pleased we were going on first. Our equipment was set up in front of theirs and when we finished our show it would be removed and theirs brought forward. We waited in our dressing room as the audience started to fill the venue. Phil and Don Everly, after twenty years working together and having a string of worldwide hits, were at this moment in time not talking to each other. This dispute went on for a number of years and I witnessed this first hand. The Losers played their debut to an enthusiastic audience who enjoyed our cover songs of American hits and loved our English accents. Americans love English accents and every American wanted to know if you lived near The Beatles, The Rolling Stones or Joe Cocker. Every American had a relative in Liverpool or was Scottish and embraced you as a long lost brother or sister.

Phil and Don arrived in separate American limousines (still not talking.) They were staying in separate hotels and insisted on separate dressing rooms in the club. Phil arrived in sports jacket and trousers and Don in denims and bare feet, with a young lady escort. Their band took to the stage, playing a couple of country rock numbers and introduced The Everly Brothers' father who came on stage and opened the show playing blue grass banjo. He was a cross between Wild Bill Hickok and Colonel Saunders with his long blonde flowing hair and moustache and beard to match. He was well into his seventies and brought the house down. We then waited for the main attraction, as Phil and Don, in their black suits with black guitars, turned around to face the audience, put their heads together in their familiar style, smiled at each other and went into 'When Will I Be Loved.' I thought, 'That's show business' and what's more, not brotherly love but brotherly lolly! They sang and performed together, did a one hour show and left separately to do it all again – still not talking to each other. Apparently, they resolved their disputes in the years to come.

This was my first night of proper show biz, playing to over five hundred people in a top class cabaret theatre. I liked it. The feeling was good. The band played well and we had a good show. Later, I would be more involved in the performance of the band, and that would lead me to comedy.

Chapter 8

Up the Kaiser

That year, 1970, we had a few more shows around the Frankfurt area and enjoyed unwinding through the early hours of the Frankfurt mornings down the Kaiser-Strasse which was the Soho of the city. John Bell knew all the clubs which were alive with live bands, prostitutes and everyone else who spent all night drinking and taking drugs. Musicians of all nationalities would get up and play. Women of the night would be performing oral sex discreetly under the tables, biting into your Bratwurst and French fries. Their delights were served all through the night with kebabs and other delicacies! Plenty of German beer would be drunk. Great music was played; jazz, funk, blues and rock n roll. We would leave as the dawn greeted the streets of Frankfurt and we retired to our beds at the Munchen-Hof.

One night the band wasn't working and we had a phone call from the group's manager asking if we would like to meet at a hotel near Frankfurt Airport where Panam and Trans-Atlantic air stewardesses stayed. Jeff, our manager, and John Bell had frequented these premises many times and dated a lot of these stewardesses who loved to party. They would fly into Frankfurt from all over the world, sometimes on long haul, fifteen hour flights, pop a couple of uppers and stay out all night before flying again the next day. Jeff was a very canny lad and had a private telephone number to the air crew arrival desk. The girls had given him this number which was top security and he would ask what stewardesses were arriving at what times from which destinations. He pretended he was a brother or family member and got away with it. He had a list and schedule of the girls and would tick them off, rating them on performance and who did the business.

This particular evening he didn't expect any of his favourites but suggested we go to their hotel just in case we might voyeur some new girls for his portfolio. The hotel bar was dead apart from one lonely looking female in the corner drinking alone. The lights were dim and not until she smiled at all four of us with green teeth did we realise she was a hooker. Jeff and John decided for an evening's sport she could have us all for $20 dollars ($5 each), about £3.50 per man. We all had to participate and the one who didn't do the business with this Arabian goddess had to pay the full $20. Jeff would call her across, buy her a drink and on a quiet Monday night with no early trade she should accept the offer and terms of business. We gradually got her pissed and Jeff stood up to dance with her to the background music playing in the bar. He whispered in her ear and suggested they go to his flat. He left the bar in his car and we three followed behind in the transit. Once there she drank everything in sight apart from the bath water. (I don't think she had ever seen a bath, never mind water in it) We noticed a grey shadow above her top lip where she shaved but she didn't bother with her legs which you could have combed.

As the group manager, always making decisions for the rest of us, Jeff took her into his bedroom and after ten minutes opened the door holding his underpants in his hands. Fifteen love! Next one to serve was John Bell. He was the same size as Jeff and was advised that in the dark she wouldn't know the difference. So, like three giggling schoolboys from Greyfriars School standing outside the headmaster's office, we slapped John Bell on the back for good luck as he entered the dark mystery of this Turkish Delight (she was either Turkish or Arabian – who knows?) Once again, ten minutes passed (this seemed to be the allotted time) and John came skipping out of the bedroom with a grin as wide as the M1, nearly choking as he quietly tried to conceal his laughter and conquest. Thirty love! Two more serves and it was game set and match. I was beginning to feel a little anxious at this stage, wondering how I was going to fit in this sequence of events but nevertheless, laughing with the other bastards as I was told Richard was next and I would be sloppy fourth. What a thought. It would be like pushing a jelly baby into a one armed bandit by the time I got there.

Richard, in his Errol Flynn manner, crept in and showed her his rapier. She apparently took it from behind and reaching a climax he swung off the chandelier onto next door's balcony and into the hallway where the Three Musketeers waited. 'One for all and all for one,' they chanted as they pushed me through the door now ajar, with light coming from within. Seconds later, in my mind I had decided to forfeit the bet and give the boys $20. But this wasn't acceptable now because they had changed the ground rules and decided a 'good shagging' was what I needed. They slammed the door and held it from the other side so I couldn't escape. She had switched the light on by now and gone for a wee. I stood like Uriah Heap, humble in the doorway. 'How many men have I been with tonight?' she asked me, lighting a fag. 'I don't know, 'I said. 'I've just come in the building, but there are three outside' (I could hear their sniggers on the other side of the door.) She jumped off the bed, now seemingly sober, grabbed me by the throat and pushed me on the bed. 'Have you slept with me? 'she asked. 'N-n-no, 'I stuttered. 'In that case you can stay,' she said and pulled me into the sheets and clamped her hands around my head, holding me in a head lock. I couldn't move, more to the point I daren't move. She was aggressive, strong and not in any mood to humour. I laid all night in that position, with her hands around my head as she breathed stale smoke and booze fumes out of her mouth. I could feel her hairy legs against mine. I wanted to escape, I wanted to move but I couldn't. Only in the morning as she turned over I became free. She ordered me to fetch her breakfast and I willingly brought her coffee and toast before she got straight out of bed, dressed without washing (If you know what I mean) and insisted I give her $20 dollars. She left for work and another client. I washed and went for a wee, $20 dollars lighter and returned to bed.

When the boys got up they were hysterical with laughter, thinking she had made me sleep with her all night. They presumed nobody could have laid in bed all night with a whore and not done it and gave me their $15 dollars. I didn't question this decision and took part in the discussion of my so-called ordeal as the boys asked questions and I exaggerated my experience and romanced a little (well, a bloody lot!) I thought to myself, 'My first sexual encounter with no sex!' That should go in the Guinness Book of Records.

A week later Jeff was in America and telephoned to say he had discovered a discharge dripping out of his best friend. John Bell had the same complaint so with advice from GIs on the base we were all recommended to visit a doctor who dealt with venereal disease. This was a shock because there were 'two with a drip' and 'two without' – very strange. I daren't tell them I wouldn't be participating in a visit to the clinic as there was no need. After all, they wouldn't have believed that a man could have stayed with a woman all night in bed and not done the deed. A 4'6" boy looking no more than twelve years old – that's who! (Notice I have now got younger and looking for the sympathy vote on the whys and wherefores of not shagging a lady of the night.) They wouldn't have understood that she'd befriended me in her bed so that no other gorilla could or would have sex with her again that night. All she wanted to do was sleep, keeping me in a wrestling hold so I couldn't escape. I was just her security blanket for the rest of the evening.

Reluctantly, John, Richard and I banged on the recommended doctor's door. We waited, the door opened and there he stood, a German doctor. We looked at him and never spoke a word. He gave us the once over and said, 'English musicians, kom in.' You had to laugh – but we didn't. We followed him into his surgery and received 500cc of penicillin, jabbed up each cheek of our bottoms and were told to go home and rest for twenty four hours. Now, I don't like jabs at the best of times even when I need one but to have one when I didn't need one, it just shows you. All that needless worry for twenty dollars and at the end of it, a German prick!

Chapter 9

Wall to Wall

The following day, with sore bottoms and no sympathy from the girls in the band who thought the whole thing was hilarious, we set off in our red transit for a gig in Berlin at a venue called The Starlight Grove in the American/British sector of the city. To get to this venue we had to travel through East Germany and then back into West Germany before arriving in Berlin. It was the Christmas holidays and the Germans had loaded up their cars to visit relatives, some going to the East and some going to the West. Thousands of families had been separated when the Berlin wall had been built in 1961 and Christmas was the only holiday period when they were allowed to visit each other. Hundreds of people a day were passing through Checkpoint Charlie and this very humiliating experience to gain access to their loved ones.

We arrived early in the morning at the checkpoint and waited in line with other cars moving very slowly towards the barrier to present our papers. Our van had English number plates and right hand drive and we stuck out like a jam pot with five bees inside. As we got closer to the checkpoint, the van was noticed by the guards who directed us out of line and into a garage at the side of the road. John drove into the garage onto an open caged floor and the guards closed the doors. My bottom was still sore from the German prick but this was nothing compared to the feeling of nervousness and apprehension that my arse was going through as we were ordered out of the van for an inspection. Orders and instructions were given in German and we were expected to understand what was said. All cars and vehicles that looked suspect of smuggling people from the East to the West were scrutinised by the German authorities and many vehicles were routinely pulled out of line. John Bell had never experienced this before but as we stepped out of the van he advised us to 'say nothing and crack no gags' as a lot of these young guards spoke English. My mouth was closed but my bottom was twitching like a rabbit's nose.

They went through our belongings with a fine tooth comb. They opened suitcases, screwed the backs of the 5' high pa speakers and opened guitar cases. A couple of these guards were wearing jack boots and carrying machine guns and only looked sixteen or seventeen years of age. They were East German guards and looking for people trying to cross to the West. As East Germany was a communist state they had heard no western music, seen no electric guitars, read no English newspapers, knew no pop groups and had little knowledge of Western life. They were told what to read, had one state television channel and were brought up by Russian idealism and communist teachings. These young guards were fascinated by our equipment. We showed them English and American sheet music and pictures of pop stars and one of them asked if he could strum a guitar. They had mirrors on long trolleys which they pushed underneath the van because people were often hidden underneath car chassis as they hung underneath vehicles, trying to escape from East to West.

There is a museum in Berlin showing pictures of different escape attempts. One man built a concrete false floor under his car and put his wife and kids in it and drove through the checkpoint. He escaped and was given the keys of Berlin City for his bravery. Other people tried to get through the checkpoint, made it through in various ways but were then shot and killed in the space between the East and West which was called 'No Man's Land.' They lay there and died, their bodies left to rot as they could not be retrieved by the West or the East.

When the Russians liberated Berlin in 1945 the city was divided into two sections. Families were immediately separated and the museum shows pictures of babies being thrown over the wall so they would not have to be brought up in a communist state. This was horrific but it showed how desperate East Berliners were and how much they hoped that their children would be looked after by people on the other side of the wall and adopted. Communism meant poverty and we witnessed women working on the roads in East Germany and all workers wore blue uniforms. Can you imagine that when these guards looked at us lot in jeans and western clothes, with our long hair, they couldn't believe what they had coming through the checkpoint. Many pop groups and shows travelled all over Germany but going from The West into the East and back again could and would create problems in these times of the Cold War.

That night, our passports and papers were taken from us and once again we were only spoken to in German. We waited thirty minutes until a guard returned with our documents. We were told to sit back in the van and our passports were handed out individually to each of us. John acknowledged the guard with a 'Danke-schon' (thank you) and the guard replied, 'Don't mention it'! He had never been out of the East but as in all James Bond films, the Russians all speak English. We didn't 'mention it' and were only too happy to drive our van out of the caged floor garage and head for the English/American sector of Berlin.

We entered the city in the early hours of the morning. We'd been driving for three days. Berlin is like London, enormous, and split into two sections of West and East. The streets were empty apart from the odd car and we drove for over two hours, looking for an address in the American sector called Paris Strasse. I remember the roads were wet and dimly lit and we were all very tired. John Bell turned a corner down yet another street and as we drove along found that this was a dead end. At the bottom of this road, with only five to ten seconds to spare for us to stop, stood the Berlin Wall and we were driving straight at it! Spotlights immediately came on as John swerved the van around and headed down a left side street. Another second and we could have been machine gun fodder if they'd thought that we were trying to ram the wall. Choice phrases such as 'flippin' heck,' 'Did you see that?' and 'Oh dear!' were expressed as we detoured, stopped the van and wiped the stains from our underpants. The girls were asleep in the back and never heard a thing. You could imagine the headlines the next day in the Berlin Gazette. 'ENGLISH BAND COMMIT SUICIDE GOING UP THE WALL IN TRANSIT VAN'!

Our next port of call, Paris Strasse, had been a very affluent Jewish part of Berlin before the war. The area had been rich with Jewish businesses. Most Jewish men and many families had been removed from these buildings and sent to the labour camps but some women and children had survived. One lady who was left was the owner of the building we were to stay in. She was called Madame Zastrow, now a lady in her mid-sixties who had survived the war and had kept her home into the 1970's. The outer walls of the building were full of bullet holes and shell marks which the Jewish people had left to show the world what they had suffered. As you entered, the walls inside were painted brown and a dim light bulb shone twenty four hours a day in the foyer because no daylight entered the building. The original pre-war caged lift had old iron doors which had to be pulled across to close it before it moved. This very depressing building, which had many a tale to tell from the days of extravagance, decadence and glamour was now converted into flats. It was full of Turkish and Moroccan workers who fought during the night as they negotiated drug deals stabbing and often killing each other in the process.

We entered the house sheepishly half laughing, got into the lift and slowly ascended to one of the floors in the building. We could hear screams and shouting and quickly shut the lift as we crept along the brown corridor lit with a bulb cased in wire netting. I had only seen this kind of thing in films set in the Bronx in New York; now I was part of it, waiting any minute to be mugged, raped or shot, not necessarily in that order. We opened our apartment door and bolted it in haste. The girls had been picked up earlier and were staying with GI's somewhere so that was a blessing; we couldn't have put up with them screaming through the night. At least us boys had only our three souls to worry about. The apartment was enormous with a huge sitting room and two bedrooms. Richard and I shared one bedroom and slept together in a large double bed through fear. John Bell always slept on his own in a 'filth pit' wallowing in his dirty clothes and smelly sheets. This suited him and it suited Richard and me. The decor of this apartment was gloomy and the rooms were filled with furniture from the war. Old, badly decaying chairs and a settee stood with the material fraying on the arms and seats. We couldn't believe our eyes when we saw in the corner of the settee, two cushions, worn and faded, with swastikas stitched into the pattern. On the walls were very old pictures, one of a young girl whose eyes followed us all around the room. I think behind her pupils were two spy holes cut out of the canvas so the Germans could spy on people in the house. Richard and I only ever looked at that picture from a distance – we were shit scared to go near it!

We both slept in that double bed and because of the noises of the house, such as the caged lift going up and down all night, voices whispering, screaming and gun shots, we probably slept in shifts, gripping our tooth brushes to use as a deterrent against any violent attacks that might come our way during the night. We blocked the door with an armchair and sideboard.

John Bell laughed the whole thing off, went to his bedroom, removed the clothes he had been wearing for the last three days and without washing, donned a red velvet suit and cherry red patent shoes and took the van for a night out in Berlin to party into the early hours. Richard and I couldn't believe the stamina of this man. John was twenty six years old and a full time stud and playboy. He drank Heineken beer for breakfast, slept only four to six hours a day and could stay up all night after driving for three days. He could mend a Perkins Diesel Transit engine with spluttering fuel injectors using a wire coat hanger. Covered in oil and diesel, he would spit on his head of curly hair, shine his boots on the back of his trousers and was ready for any action the world threw at him. He laughed and joked at every event and never found fault with anyone.

Richard and I watched him leave the apartment that first night with a spring in his step as we gingerly climbed into the double bed, looking at the girl on the wall looking back at us. Then we moved around the room to see if her eyes followed us. 'Yes,' said Richard, 'they do'. We kept the light on all night, pushed the furniture back near the door and sat smoking and nervously waiting for what fate the night would have in store for us.

We must have slept a little because around the first signs of daylight we heard the lift moving and John's voice laughing and joking, speaking to a woman. He was assuring her in the corridor that he was the only person living here and she agreed to come in. Richard and I scurried to the door, moved the chair and lifted the sideboard away, switched off the light and ran back into bed and hid under the covers.

John and his new found love with an American accent were drunk. They giggled and laughed before entering his bedroom and he left the door open. She didn't know Richard and I were in the second bedroom, listening like two schoolboys, slapping each other under the sheets as John proceeded to make mad passionate love to this girl. Now, Richard and I couldn't see this master class in seduction but we heard history being made as she straddled his gear stick. By now I was biting the pillow to restrain myself from laughing and Richard had his back towards me, elbowing my sides. By the sounds of what was happening and John's comments on the subject, she was making a fabulous job of shagging him on top. Then suddenly, without warning, their bed collapsed and a leg fell off, jettisoning the lovers onto the floor, still remaining in their compromising position. Richard bellowed with laughter and I went into a spasmodic fit similar to the girl possessed in The Exorcist, throwing myself off the bed. John went into fits of raucous laughter like a wounded hyena. The young lady screamed and jumped off the bed and picked up her items of clothing as John tried to console her and make light of the situation. Remember, this apartment was pitch black inside and she was genuinely very frightened. Richard and I sat on the end of our bed with our heads in our hands and John hurried his young lady into the bathroom where she got dressed and left the apartment in a hurry. We heard John trying to ease the situation but she shouted, 'You fucking sick Limey!' He escorted her to the lift and came back wiping the tears of laughter from his face.

The next day we stood Madame Zastrow's bed on its broken leg, collected the girls and headed for the Starlight Grove lounge to do our last show. After the gig we drove back through the night and another twenty four hour trip back to Frankfurt.

Chapter 10

Three Minute Warnings

The Plantation Club was on the base of the 97th Military Hospital in Frankfurt. We were now going to be the resident band for a month. We worked six nights a week and performed four forty five minute spots on a weekday and five on a Saturday. This included our cabaret spots. The GI's would flock around Norma and Lesley and try and date them. The girls had their pick of them and they enjoyed the attention and money the Americans spent on them. Americans are very generous people and trays of drinks were sent to the stage after every spot so by the end of the evening we were warmed up for the after show entertainment down town!

We arrived at the Military Hospital on a very quiet Sunday afternoon. It was very warm and the sun was shining. All bases in Germany were supposed to be on High Security Alert due to the bombing of American installations by the Baader Meinhof, a socialist German Organisation in disagreement with the Americans' presence in Vietnam and using Germany as an ally to train and send troops to this war. They had bombed quite a few American bases and killed their servicemen. It was national news at the time and security was top priority – or so we had been led to believe. We drove up to the main gate and there stood an empty sentry box with a rifle propped up alongside it. Six feet away, sitting on the ground, was a black American soldier on guard. He was in full battledress and wearing purple beads around his neck and purple shades to match. He stood up slowly, walked over to us and uttered that all-American familiar phrase of greeting, 'Hey, what's happening man?' 'We're the band,' John replied. 'Ride on man,' said the guard. 'D' ya play James Brown? Got any shit?'

He was guarding the whole place against terrorist attack. He couldn't give a shit who came in or went out. He was as high as a kite as he puffed on a joint he'd held behind his back.

'Okay y' all. I'm supposed to check out the van, so open the doors. Man, y'all from England? Hey, that's cool. Y'all know Joe Cocker?' He opened the van doors and seeing it was stacked to the roof with equipment, shut it again, took another drag on his joint and waved us through.

These boys had had no intention of being called up, sent to Germany or any other part of the world to do National Service. Some had been drug dealers, gangsters; others bankers, Texas ranchers, doctors and lawyers. Nixon was in power and the National Guard had been sent out all over the States to the student protests against the Vietnam War. In The US, blacks, whites, Italians, Puerto Ricans and any other male Americans over seventeen years of age, fit and well, were called up for National service. The American Military put every nationality and every background, rich and poor together to fight this war. In the States, blacks and whites were segregated but not in Europe. Especially In Germany they were put together. Some Texans had never walked on the same side of the street as a black man, never sat on the same bus. Now here they shared the same barracks, shared the same clubs, trained together and shared the same women. The black guys charmed the knickers off the German girls and for most of them to get a white girl, well – this was something else! The white GI's took badly to this and called the German girls whores. It was a novelty for the German girls as well, because there weren't many black guys in Germany before the bases were established and they loved their fancy clothes, big hats and colourful suits. These men had money and cars here and a chance of showing off and being equal in another country. They spent their money on the white girls and obviously it was a breeding ground for prostitution. Where there are men in great numbers you will find girls wanting to sell sex. In cities such as Frankfurt, Hamburg and Nuremberg there were large streets full of girls selling their bodies.

Joey Who?

The Military got paid twice a month and would go window shopping for sex on payday. Now, when I say 'window shopping' it was just like Amsterdam today. That's how it was in the seventies. In Nuremberg, girls sat in windows on chairs, on beds, across furniture, in every seductive position to entice the GI's and relieve them of their wages. Through the night the guys would arrive on bikes, in jeeps and taxis, ready to spend their pay packets on these beauties of the night. Depending on how much you wanted to spend, this determined the quality and class of your whore. At the beginning of the street there were ladies and girls from sixteen to thirty five, seductively dressed in leather and PVC, in basques and stockings to sophisticated evening dress and gloves. What you chose depended on your money, personal taste and what you saw in the window. As you passed further down the street the standard became lower and lower until you hit rock bottom with fifty to sixty year old 'ladies' sitting on a step with no knickers on!

The GI's would go at it hammer and tongs through the evening and early morning until around 4 or 5 a.m. when business had died off. Across the other side of the road at this time of night would congregate Turks, Moroccans, Africans and anyone else who wanted to dip his wick before dawn. They would wait with eagerness as the girls and old ladies would signal them across the road with a wink and the gesture of a cigarette to go and fill their boots. We went there on several occasions after a night on the German ale to watch and laugh in amazement at this Circus of Sex. Guys would only take in the correct money at the going rate and leave their wallets with their pals outside because due to past experience while on the job in these ladies' bedrooms, the pimp would come in behind them, nick the money out of their clothes and then beat them up. Many a night I stood on the pavement holding Richard's coat and wallet as he fell out of the 'Hole in the Wall Bank' He had only spent $10 but had deposited a lot more! We agreed that all banks should be open between 4 a.m. and 5 a.m. You got a better rate of interest and for a small withdrawal you could put in what you liked and quickly take it out. I was not a client of 'The Sperm Bank' and I was frightened that I didn't have enough to put in! That was Nuremberg where they later tried the war criminals. It was also where the American military tried every woman in sight.

One day, whilst rehearsing at the Plantation club in the morning, a three minute warning was alerted on the base. This could happen at any time and was a drill against a Russian attack in Europe. The complete base, as many as three to five thousand people, had to be ready for combat in three minutes. There were tanks revving, convoys of trucks loaded with troops and on the Air bases, fighter squadrons ready for takeoff in minutes. It was organised chaos and we witnessed this several times over two years at different bases we worked on.

When the sirens went off, every GI would immediately assemble in full combat gear at his station. One day we were rehearsing James Brown's 'Sex Machine' and heard the sirens but didn't realise what was going on so we continued to play, drowning out the noise with our music. As civilians, nobody had warned us of this alert and we assumed it was just another drill of some kind so we continued rehearsing in the empty club. Outside, jeeps, lorries and armoured vehicles were moving into position as personnel alerted themselves. Around six black GI's walked past the club in no hurry at all. They were half dressed, buttoning up their uniforms with combat equipment slung around their necks. They were trailing their rifles behind them and made Dad's Army look like The Green Beret. One of these guys heard our music coming from inside the club and said to his pals, 'Hey man – 'Sex Machine' – James Brown'. They dropped their rifles and combat equipment and came inside and danced! 'What's happening?' we asked. 'Three minute warning shit,' one shouted. 'Keep playing man. Y'all playing real good'. This was one of the funniest things I have ever seen. We finished the song and they left the club and got dressed, still dancing after giving us a high five.

The alert was a drill and the base came back to normal later that day.

The guys came to the club many times, brought their friends and as 'white British dudes' they enjoyed us playing American soul music. Now, this club was predominantly black; other places were predominantly white, full of Texans. No soul music played there – just country. We had to be versatile, as most bands were, and cater for every type of GI. In some venues, when it was mixed, we would start off with soul and then you would hear from the bar, 'Don't give us any of that nigger shit, play Johnny Cash.' So not wanting to offend we changed from James Brown's 'Hot Pants' to 'Folsom Prison Blues' in the same song. Then the black guys would shout, 'Hey man, make it funky, play some soul.' We didn't want to upset the gangsters and the mob from Chicago who sometimes were 'packing a piece' in their trousers (a gun down the back of their Y fronts). So John would shout, 'No problem man,' as he conducted the band from 'Walk the line' to 'Dance to the Music', Sly and the Family Stone. Then all hell broke loose as the white guys started to fight with the black guys. As usual, we carried on playing until the military police were alerted and cleared the club with the help of riot sticks and police dogs. The club would be closed and opened again ten minutes later for us to start playing once again. It was like Gunfight at the OK Corral; chairs thrown, glasses smashed and guys badly injured. Our girls in the band were very frightened and would leave the stage for Richard to play a ten minute blues or rock solo from Santana, Led Zeppelin or Eric Clapton that would usually please everybody and we would finish our set until the next fight. We would calm the mood sometimes and stick in a comedy sketch or routine and bring the girls back on stage. This would ease the tension as we got the guys laughing as they wiped the blood and guts from the tables and chairs.

I got involved in the comedy and the more laughs I got the more I came off the drums. I enjoyed being out front and became part of the routines. People laughed and I enjoyed the feeling this gave. This was to become my forte for the future. My passion at this time was still the drums and even today, forty five years on, I would have loved to have played music and do big concerts. Drummers are always drummers and I still tap all day long on most surfaces that sound good. I have played with every band in the world from rock, soul, blues and country as I listen to the radio sitting in the bath, giving it four beats to the bar with my loofah.

The standard of the groups playing on the American Military circuit was top class. One of my favourite bands was Rhine River Union. They were a German and Indonesian group and were such a tight unit and excellent musicians. Their set would go from Santana, playing all the percussion to five part harmony Ink Spots around the mike and then into Jimi Hendrix. Another band we saw at a showcase (where acts audition for work) was a band from America called Johnny Green and the Green men. They played instruments, did magic, illusions and fire eating and generally stole the show. They were dressed in green suits, had green lighting and green hair. Yes, green hair! They were a sensational show and everybody wanted to book them. 'Right that's it,' we said. 'We'll do it in blue'. We bought blue suits and had our hair done the same colour blue. Now, as every hairdresser will know, that to dye your hair any colour, first you must go peroxide blonde and then the colour rinse goes on top. We booked into a Frankfurt hairdressing salon and had the works. The blue rinse looked great for two weeks and then after several washes it needed doing again. When you are on the road travelling, the nearest hairdresser would have to take on this mega task and for five of us having it done at different times by different salons, I can only describe the result as 'Worzel Gummidge'. The blue gradually goes green unless it's done regularly and the yellow peroxide starts to come through with the black roots showing. We couldn't keep up with the two weekly appointments or the cost which in those days would have been around £20/£30 a time.

Walking through Sunderland one day on a trip back home and after doing some gigs in the northern clubs instead of looking fabulous for the working class audiences of the North, the general opinion was, 'What a sad set of silly looking bastards'. One day, we passed a ladies hairdresser's and the girls in the shop, together with the clients, pulled back the curtains to laugh at us. This was the 'last straw' quite literally as our dead ends were breaking off, so we bit the bullet and went into the shop and had it all cut off. The girls and clients thought we were pop stars and screamed when we entered the shop. Well, that's what they said!

That was August and we had come back to England for four weeks. I had been writing to Kathy all the time I was away and she was very happy to see me with my normal hair after witnessing it blue, green and a mucky yellow. She was still very much in love with me and had come away on several holidays in the last year I was with the band. I had sent her postcards from every place we visited and she religiously kept a scrapbook of our pictures and cuttings.

After keeping our finances afloat for the month, working clubs and cabaret in England, the band was booked back in Germany and we continued playing to the American military until Christmas. We came home for Christmas and got ready to travel to Zaragoza near Madrid for New Year's Eve at the Air Force base there.

The poor old red transit van couldn't cough up another German autobahn or climb the Austrian Alps anymore. John Bell's days of cleaning the fuel injector pipes by ramming them with a wire coat hanger had gone. On one occasion the brakes failed and Richard and John slid open the side doors and jumped out as it coasted down a hill, leaving me sitting in the passenger seat with brown lumps ready to appear in my trousers as the smell of death lingered around my bottom region. Telling God how much I loved Him and that I would never be a shit again in my life, the van cruised onto some flat road and grabbing the wheel, I steered her to a halt. John and Richard were rolling on the road in guffaws of laughter as my white face and badly soiled trousers walked away from the van declaring that I would never set foot in it again. The girls were frightened when we travelled in it and now that it was becoming unreliable on a daily basis. Enough was enough.

However, John arrived in Hull for our departure to Spain in a large Vauxhall V10 saloon car pulling a horse box. Yes, a horse box! We asked, 'Where's the horse?' John assured us that this was now the way to travel. 'Comfort in the car and all the equipment in the horse box,' he said, plus we could leave the box anywhere and travel in style. The car had leather seats and plenty of room. The girls were very impressed and Richard and I could sleep all day in the back!

Chapter 11

Snowbound to Spain

A week later, on December 28th 1970 we boarded the ferry for Rotterdam once again and I endured the crossing by kissing Ralph and Huey at every opportunity until we reached Holland. We planned to arrive in Spain for the show on the 30th – plenty of time to get ready for New Year's Eve. Our lifestyle had become that of travellers, moving from country to country, city to city and usually arriving five to six hours before show time. We ate and drank when we could and begged meals and booze from every available fan or hotel that would provide us with them for free. John would top up his daily supply of Heineken and we would set off again in the luxury of our Vauxhall V10 and horsebox which was packed to the gunnels. Remember the Beverley Hillbillies? Say no more!

As we travelled through Holland and France and approached the borders of Spain it started to snow. The weather got worse and as we approached the Pyrenees Mountains, which we had to cross, advice was given to turn back in these conditions – especially with a large saloon car and a horsebox loaded to the gunnels! Cars were passing us with chains on their wheels and skis on bonnets and roof racks ready for a pleasant holiday in the snow-capped mountains. We had five people in our car and were pulling a small shed. Italians and Spanish tourists were beeping their horns as they passed us, slowly climbing up the very narrow winding pass. We climbed several thousand feet, the snow getting thicker and the car wheels spinning and skidding at every turn. But we had started now so we couldn't turn back. We had travelled nonstop for two days. The car and horse box together were too long to turn round and the road wasn't wide enough. As we gently crawled, traffic behind us was building up and very frustrated drivers waved welcoming hand signals at this crazy English saloon car pulling a large aluminium dustbin on wheels. We came to a bend and John gave the steering wheel full lock to sweep the horsebox round, but the bend was too tight. The horsebox's rear end skidded, came off the road and jack knifed, hanging six feet over the mountainside. Luckily, I was wearing my brown trousers this time. I didn't want to go through that again.

The girls screamed and John slammed on the handbrake. The weight of the box was heavier than the car, even with us five in it and if we moved the whole lot could go over the side. We were now blocking the turn in the road. The passengers in the cars behind got out of their vehicles and tried to push us free. John lifted the handbrake off and felt the clutch plates stick together from the red hot metal as we listened to the engine revving and screaming. We were stuck, completely blocking traffic both ways (in deep shit and deep snow). Foreigners were shouting at us in Spanish and Italian and with hand gestures and poking of chests they indicated that a snowplough was coming from the opposite direction. The driver could pull the car and the horsebox to safety and make a path around the road so vehicles could pass.

John carefully slid his body from behind the steering wheel and went to find the snow plough driver, as surrounding tourists held onto the back end of the box. The drop off the road wasn't visible because of the blizzard conditions but we were several thousand feet above sea level and once again, on the precipice of death. The Famous Five didn't want to die. We had lived through numerous North Sea crossings. We had lived through Berlin. We had lived through doses of clap. We had lived through American saloon gun fights. We had lived through three minute warnings against Russia. We had survived playing country music in soul clubs. I didn't want to go over a Spanish mountainside in a Vauxhall V10 dragged by a horsebox full of amplifiers, guitars, speakers and a drum kit plus five suitcases with blue suits inside!

John returned thirty minutes later to inform us that the snow plough driver was having his siesta and when he'd finished he wanted 5,000 pesetas (around £200) to come and pull us free. This went down a treat, what with the drivers both ways not going anywhere and now, a tailback the length of Land's End to John O'Groat's! The road was only just wide enough for one lane each side and even the Police couldn't get through to organise the chaos, which was getting worse by the minute.

Remember, in those days, there were no mobile phones, and here there was only a desolate Spanish phone box three miles away, covered in snow and ice and not working in this blizzard. So by word of mouth, people passed messages from car to car. John made a decision to pay the snowplough driver and we had a whip round for the money (Yes – you've guessed it – 1,000 pesetas each!) He marched off again with help and encouragement from his newfound friends, the irate car drivers from behind. While this was happening the four of us sat in the car, motionless, to keep the weight balanced in case we slipped over the edge or were lynched by skiers who thought they would never see the piste again.

Ten minutes went by before we saw the snow plough pushing through, making a track through six feet of snow, doing a detour around the cars on the opposite side of the road. John sat in the cab with his new friend, 'El Twato', the richest snow plough driver this side of Madrid. The plough sucked the snow in from the front and shot it out through two funnels into the air each side of the road. We sat, still not daring to move in the car, with by then, a group of tourists perched on the car bonnet, keeping the weight on our side. El Twato came as close as the snow and gap would allow and attaching a chain to the car's towing hook he pulled us and the horse box clear and into the clearing he had made in the snow.

The Spanish and Italians cheered and so did any other nationality that witnessed the day's event. It was similar to Apollo 13 landing in the sea when the capsule door was opened from the outside and the astronauts emerged safe with a smile and a wave. Four of us emerged, well, crawled out of the car to shouts of 'Get a fucking move on!'

'Clear the road!' and 'English bastards!' mostly in Italian and Spanish, which may I add, was a great comfort to us all. John went and sat in the bushes alone waiting for the car's clutch plates to separate and cool down. El Twato unchained us, moved off and our short-lived European friends of the day drove around us waving and wishing us 'all the best' in their native tongues. We waved back and returned the gesture with Winston Churchill's victory sign and 'Fuck you too'!

We had never seen John so deflated as he was that day and the girls had to console him. He had only bought the car a week ago and if the clutch had burnt out we were in deep shit, up the mountains without transport and a booking on New Year's Eve we couldn't honour. Also, the problem of getting it fixed half way up the Pyrenees. After twenty minutes waving goodbye to onlookers we sat back in the car and discussed our fate. Everyone has an idea better than yours in a crisis until the arguments start, don't they? 'Whose fault is it?', 'Who got us in this mess?' and 'Fuck all of you, I'm leaving the band! On that day we would all have liked to leave the band, but we couldn't, not half way up the Pyrenees with no wheels and no clutch. John, now with ice hanging from his moustache after sitting outside in the trees contemplating suicide, decided to join us in the car and try the clutch once more. He turned the key again and pressed the clutch pedal down. Now, in all good films it usually takes three attempts for anything to work, but after pushing and moving the gear stick several times the clutch plates separated and pressing his foot to the floor, John found his gears. We had take off! Just like Flight of the Phoenix but we didn't strap ourselves to the aeroplane wings, we slapped and smacked each other around the head and shoulders as John turned over the engine. With a clunk of the gearstick we set off once again up the mountain pass with all four of us joining the band again. I'd asked John one day, 'Why are we called The Losers Showband' and he replied 'Can't you guess?' The journey for the next twelve hours was treacherous and travelling at around forty miles an hour for another 450 miles we arrived at the base at midday December 31st. I don't remember the gig – too much booze!

We stayed in Spain until the summer and came home to have our roots done. While we were at home John Bell contacted each member of the band by telephone and told us he'd made a decision not to go back abroad and to disband The Losers. He explained that funds had been cut from the military budgets for entertainment and he was going to be a road manager, travelling around the world with top American acts. He had had enough. Deep down we'd all had enough, really. The end was nigh and it was only time before we would split up. The girls were sick of touring and were looking for more stable relationships. John had been with The Losers for over eleven years and 'didn't want to Lose' anymore. Richard and I went home. We had spent the last eighteen months together every day. Sleeping, eating, travelling, rehearsing and performing together. We were ready for a break. Richard went back to Lincoln and I came back to Hull.

Both Richard and I found it quite hard to adapt to normal family life. He went to work in a man's boutique and formed his own band with brass, playing soul music. I tried several daytime jobs. A milkman for a week, lifting milk crates off a lorry onto milk floats up and down the East coast of England while the driver of the lorry sat in his cab and rolled fags. Up at 3 a.m. every morning and getting £12 per week. I was earning £12 for two nights drumming in the clubs, backing acts on a night. So when the manager of the milk depot asked why I couldn't get up in a morning I told him it was because I was drumming until midnight in the clubs and pubs of Hull. So he gave me an ultimatum. 'You're going to have to decide if you want to be a drummer or a milkman.' After three sleepless nights and a long walk in the park contemplating my future... Well, he hadn't got the words out of his mouth before I told him to 'shove your pint bottles of full cream milk past your eyes' (pasteurised) and to sterilise himself with a gold top. My wages were sent to the office and I left – homogenised! Working for others was not my cup of tea. I had travelled through Europe, seen all aspects of life and didn't want to be ordered about by a two bit manager or lorry driver in a brown coat whose life was a cheese sandwich every day at 12 o'clock and two weeks holiday once a year in Cleethorpes. I found that most men in these managerial jobs in the workplace or at night such as the concert chairman at the club, were 'Little Hitlers': Power mad, never been anywhere, never done anything, 'the jobsworth' of a post war society. I resigned myself to the fact I would play in the clubs and look for a new drumming job as soon as possible.

Chapter 12

An Apple a Day

Over the next few weeks I looked in The New Musical Express music paper at the 'Job Vacancies' column: 'Musicians wanted'. When I saw 'DRUMMER REQUIRED FOR TOP TEN POP GROUP', I applied and waited a week or more.

I had been working at The Hull Transport Club playing drums with Rosemary Lilley, the organist there. We were a cross between Focus and Emerson Lake and Palmer – more like Hinge and Brackett! Rose was a music student and wore white plastic knee length boots. She had a large handbag and complemented her outfit with different pinafore dresses and spectacles. She played the Lowry organ a dream and jazz, pop and classics were performed to perfection as the club audience formed a queue for their bingo tickets! Rose never took her boots off and in the three months I worked with her she never had a change of shoes. I imagined her feet on fire and smoke rising out the top of her boots as she moved her legs vigorously to and fro up and down the organ bass pedals.

A couple of weeks later, I remember sitting on the stairs of my mother's hallway waiting for a call from a Bill Collins who had rung whilst I was at work and told my mother he would ring back at around 11 p.m. that night.

I sat on the stairs and true to his word, the phone went at 11p.m. and a voice with a Liverpool accent asked if I was Howard and we chatted for over thirty minutes. Bill was the father of Lewis Collins, the television actor. He managed the pop group Badfinger. Together with Mary Hopkin, they were the first signings of new artists on Apple Records. The Beatles owned Apple and Badfinger had reached global success with three top ten hits; 'If you want it here it is, come and get it', 'No Matter What You Are' and 'Day After Day'. They'd had hits in major countries all over the world and had top selling albums. I couldn't believe what I was hearing. I loved the band; they were a protégé of Paul McCartney and John Lennon and sang great harmonies and played excellent guitar. Three hundred replies had been sent in to the advertisement, the band had picked thirty to audition and I was included in those. Bill asked me If I would like to go to Denmark Street's Tinpan Alley in London the following Friday and do the audition with the band. They would be seeing drummers every day from Monday to Friday. Would I? I told him I couldn't make Friday due to flower arranging classes at the local church... I booked a seat from Hull to Kings Cross station for the next Friday afternoon.

In the meantime, I went to the local record shop and bought Badfinger's albums and practised like mad in my mother's front room, drumming on two cushions on her three piece suite. Cushions make good silent drums and you can play to your heart's contents without annoying your dad, mother and neighbours. By the time I went to London, I knew all their songs backwards. Kathy was pleased for me but a little worried about what this could bring. After all, she had spent the last eighteen months alone but she assured me she was prepared to be a musician's widow once again. My mother and father didn't realise how big the band was and my dad thought I should be looking for a 'proper job' instead of 'buggering about drumming'!

Donning a blue leather suit with bright red lapels and cuffs (bought during the Losers days). I nervously travelled to the big city. I ventured on the train to Kings Cross then took a taxi to Denmark Street. Tin Pan Alley was the centre of the London music industry at that time. Elton John started there, working for Dick James Music in his office. Everyone who has been someone, from the Beatles to the Stones to Queen have sat and discussed their next hit over a coffee down this world famous back street.

My audition was around 8 pm. I walked into an upstairs rehearsal room above a pub. The room was about twenty feet square with wall to wall speakers. The boys in the band had been auditioning drummers all week and were sick of seeing them. They had cans of beer on top of the amplifiers and ashtrays full of cigarettes as they were literally chain smoking. They were dressed in tee shirts, unshaven and mentally and physically exhausted. I walked in, this little Yorkshire lad in a blue and red leather suit full of zips and 12" bottom flares. I was in awe meeting them and recognised all three of them from Top of the Pops and their album covers. They were polite to me and pointed me to the drum kit provided. Because I was so small I had taken the blocks off my three wheeler bike and attached them to the high-hat and bass drum pedal. I adjusted the kit so I could reach the drums and cymbals and they announced what we would play. I knew all three numbers we went through and laid those drumsticks down like a blacksmith hitting an anvil. Now, although I was small in stature and had arms the width of twiglets, I had power and I could 'lay it down'. I played the songs with vibrancy and gusto and gained a nod of approval from the lads. Bill was very friendly and after we'd finished he uttered those immortal words, 'We will be in touch'. I got another taxi back to Kings Cross and sat pondering on the train back to Hull, the question, 'Could I handle being a Pop star?' I had played to the best of my ability, not put a foot wrong, maybe too chatty, but I had made Bill Collins laugh and I think he liked me.

I waited for the touch for two weeks and then got another call to ask if I could come again? I told Bill it depended on what day as I attended metal work classes once a week to build up my' scrawny arms'. He said the boys had liked me and he would collect me from Kings Cross, this time in a 4 x 4 Land Rover. They wanted me to stay with them at their house in Golders Green the next weekend and record at Apple. What! I explained I would be forfeiting two nights playing at The Hull Transport Club with Rosemary and losing a fee of £12, for a weekend in London with Badfinger and recording at Apple. Bill, with his Scouse sense of humour, laughed at the gag and explained if I got the job, I wouldn't have to worry about the £12 as the wages for the drummer were £1,700 a week! The new drummer would have to be ready for an Australian tour in three weeks. I couldn't take all this in. Apple recording, Australia, money that you would only win on the pools.

I was to bring my own drum kit and record on the Saturday at Apple. Bill would collect me from Kings Cross on the Friday afternoon, I'd have a day with the boys at the house and go home on the Sunday. He pointed out that I was down to the last two; the drummer from another famous pop group of the sixties had applied and it was basically between him and me.

Well, another week of apprehension went by as I polished my Rodgers drum kit and dug out my old jeans and tee shirts to fit in with these boys for a day I will never forget at Apple. Bill picked me up from the station and took me to a lovely old Tudor house in the heart of Golders Green. It was quite sparse inside, very student-orientated and full of musical and recording equipment. There was an odd settee on floorboards with bean bags and cushions, that sort of thing. I was quite surprised. My mother's house was furnished better. You must remember I am working class and this was the early seventies. I hadn't experienced hippy or student environments. At home we had three square meals a day, a carpet on the floor and watched Coronation Street. This was alien to me. In Europe I had frequented lovely German guest houses, and American bases, all well furnished and clean. This was a bit like Woodstock without the mud! Anyway, who was I to criticize? These boys were loaded so if they didn't want a carpet, then so be it.

Bill showed me to a little guest room where I plonked my small suitcase on the floorboards and went to look round. In the main lounge stood a piano and amplifier and reel to reel recording tape machines and percussion instruments and guitars. Half of the room was boarded out to deaden the sound for recording. Bill explained that the boys put down tracks and recorded songs in the house any time of the day as and when they had ideas and inspiration. Pete Ham was lead vocalist, songwriter, guitar and piano player in the group and had written Harry Nilsson's 'Without You' in this house – and I was worried there were no carpets!

The afternoon passed and I saw no one until the evening when the band arrived with their girlfriends. Everyone was very nice to me and they drunk more beer and anything else available in the house. A man arrived in a van with a case full of fresh pineapples and the band proceeded to cut them up with a large machete and eat them, as well as smoking joints and consuming alcohol at the same time. I was offered everything but declined to partake and said I would go for a walk and have a look round. I was starving really; I didn't want pineapple, wacky baccy or booze – just some proper food. I walked down the road and came across heaven – McDonald's! I went in, filled my face and returned to the hippy house. There were around eight or nine people in there now and a little party was taking place, with guitar playing, laughter and merriment. I felt like a visitor or a fly on the wall as I watched, nodded, smiled and sat in awe of this chart topping pop group. The band was used to a lot of people around so another odd character from Yorkshire didn't make any difference. They kept offering me large hand rolled cigarettes that looked like funnels and lit up like a furnace. I declined once again. I had tried pot and things abroad but, to be honest, they had never done a thing for me apart from once in France after having a 'blow' I thought I was a bird and wanted to jump off a six floor apartment and fly. Richard told me he had a worm in his pocket and that brought me down to earth!

I settled down with another beer and after a bit of polite conversation I said goodnight and retired to my room. I couldn't sleep due to the noise downstairs and through the night it got louder as the party took on more laughter, singing and music as the boys started 'jamming' on their guitars and the piano. I woke about 10.a.m. the next morning and the house was silent. I dressed and walked downstairs to the debris of the party and decided to have another trot to McDonald's for my breakfast. Golders Green was busy with people shopping and I enjoyed seeing their vibrant community on a Saturday morning. I returned to the house and waited till four in the afternoon when the band arrived to collect me for Apple. Joey Mollander, another member of the band, drove me and his girlfriend to the studio in a brand new Lotus and I was offered refreshments and sandwiches as we waited for the rest of the band to arrive. A lovely secretary-type in a blouse and pencil skirt brought us salmon and cucumber sandwiches on a silver tray and a tobacco tin with tailor made 'joints' to smoke. Joey and his girlfriend indulged and I passed again, worried that I would either make a fool of myself or get too 'stoned' to play.

However, by 6 p.m. the full band and recording staff had arrived and I was told to assemble my drum kit in the drum booth. This is like a small area of space where screens are put around the drums to condense the sound away from the other instruments. Microphones are put close to each drum and inside the bass drum and overhead to pick up the sound made. I was then told by the producer in the sound room to tap each drum for level and tune.

After two minutes of tapping my drums, a voice from the control room shouted, 'Fucking hell, those drums sound like something from The Jungle Book! Whip the drum skins off and dampen the sound.' This meant new skins were put on my drums, they were tuned again and a mixture of black tape, cloths and polystyrene pieces were stuck to them to capture a sound that when played sounded like a set of wet brown paper bags. I thought the sound was shit. 'Does this producer know what he's doing?' I asked myself. Well, the guys put on their guitars and Pete Ham sat behind John Lennon's white piano and we proceeded to play 'Timeless', a new song. The band told me how they wanted it played and I performed as required. We did about twelve takes and then we listened to the playback. The drums sounded like a mixture of thunder and lightning. Fantastic! It was so good I didn't know it was me playing. The boys lost interest in me after that and carried on working with guitar and vocals. I had got it right. At about two in the morning they decided to finish the session and went clubbing in and around London. I was taken back to the house and with McDonald's shut, went to bed.

Bill Collins came to see me on the Sunday lunchtime and to take me back to the train. He was a lovely man. He was seventy years of age and before managing Badfinger he had looked after the Mojos, another sixties band from Liverpool who had had success a few years previously. Bill's hair was silver and shoulder length, he wore knee length boots outside his trousers and smoked a pipe. He looked like Sitting Bull. He had a girlfriend in her late twenties who called him Little Big Horn! (Well, that speaks for itself!) He asked me if I had a girlfriend and I told him about Kathy and her loyalty and support over the last two years. He understood close relationships and had been married for many years before losing his wife a few years ago. He explained that wives and girlfriends were not good for pop bands or their image. Female fans didn't like pop groups having relationships. The band had to travel all over the world and spend a lot of time in the States and he didn't like the idea of female influences in and around the band. Casual relationships were okay but the band's prime object was to write hit songs, be a global success and make money. That was 'The Name of the Game', another Badfinger song. He suggested I was far too young to have a steady relationship and this would cause doubt and uncertainty when making decisions in the future. The band came first.

I understood what he was saying and tried to convince him that Kathy wanted me to have this job and had accepted my career in the past, although she would miss me He said, 'No woman in her right mind accepts the life of a pop star and through experience, knows it finishes relationships.' If I got the job he would want me to finish with Kathy for her sake now, and that would save breaking her heart later on. I knew deep down I couldn't do this to her at this stage of my life. He made me feel uncertain about myself and very insecure. I wanted the job, but didn't want to end things with her. He understood and felt maybe I was not mature enough as a person to take on this position and I needed to think things out more before becoming a professional musician, or making a commitment to Kathy. He was right and I went home with very mixed up thoughts and feelings.

I didn't hear anything from Bill for about six weeks so took another day job in Hull and started playing in the clubs again at night. I kind of realised the job would not be given to me and read in the newspapers that the original drummer had gone back to the band and they were recording a new album. A year later Pete Ham hanged himself in his garage. Months later, Tommy Evans, the bass player, did the same. Badfinger had finished.

Chapter 13

A Home Run

I had been mostly abroad for over two years and only came home twice. I stayed at my parents' house when at home and you can imagine how awkward that was after my life of a wandering pop minstrel. I had to creep in with my key and not make a sound. I visited Kathy's house twenty minutes down the road and had a cuddle on the doorstep. Her parents, brothers and family were lovely people and treated me like a pop star. They welcomed me into the family nest.

Kathy and I carried on as boyfriend and girlfriend but we wanted to be together in our own place so we got married. She was eighteen and I was twenty. Yes, twenty. A child, a boy still in my Boy's Brigade uniform. Richard from The Losers was my best man. Kathy and I found a nice one bedroomed flat for £4 a week, above a plumber's merchants in the next street to her mother's. My father put us a breakfast bar in the kitchen which we painted orange. We decorated the lounge purple and bought a black three piece suite. We were very happy there.

Richard and I were both treading water in day jobs and semi-professional bands so we decided to form a musical comedy trio which we called Art, (Richard) Bart (Steve) & Fargo (Me) I still wanted to play the drums but fancied trying comedy again as well. The most successful acts of the day were using this combination of music and comedy: The Rockin' Berries, The Grumbleweeds, The Barron Knights, The Black Abbotts. All these top cabaret variety show groups packed venues across the country and progressed to television shows and hit records. They all had very funny front men who become established comedians and impressionists in their own right. Many took solo careers and some are still working today. I wanted to try our luck, go professional again and work throughout the British Isles. Clubland was booming. You could work seven nights a week and double at a late night cabaret if you wanted. You could see Shirley Bassey in Sheffield or Tom Jones in Newcastle, Tommy Cooper in Luton or Johnny Mathis in Manchester. Forget theatres; they were only for plays. You saw the stars in the clubs and in cabarets from Blackpool to Bradford every night of the week.

I travelled to Richard's in Lincoln and a bass player called Steve joined us. He was a very confident player and up for comedy. Richard was the musical rock and the anchor in the band. We rehearsed and put together a comedy cabaret spot of music, impressions and sketches. We wore blue three piece pin stripe suits with blue handkerchiefs in the top pockets and looked very smart. I came off the drums, did some stand-up and slowly started to feel my way as an entertainer. We had a very polished show and the audiences loved it. For the next year we worked solidly up and down the country, building up confidence and experience in different venues, from village halls, pubs and clubs to hotels, cabaret venues and the occasional 'posh do'.

One of these was a classic 'out of control self-indulgence' – commonly known as 'never get pissed before you go on'. It's not big and it's not clever. We arrived at a private members' club situated in Royal Berkshire. The venue was a cabaret restaurant on two floors in an old windmill. We got there around three in the afternoon and had to haul our equipment up the side of the windmill to the second floor with a hoist, tackle and a net. The old grain door at the side of the windmill was opened and everything came in through this door. Our show was not until ten that evening so no emphasis was given to time as we plodded on at a leisurely pace and set up around 4.30 pm.

We then had more than five hours to kill and sat in a boardroom with a drinks cabinet. After running round the board room table for ten minutes we got bored and Steve decided to look in the cabinet which wasn't locked. Steve liked a drink and could polish off a bottle of Bailey's, two pints of lager and a glass of red wine in an hour. He wasn't fussed. We had five hours! The cabinet was full of spirits, not ghosts, although Steve could enter into the paranormal and see things we couldn't after a skinful. From banana liqueur to whisky, from Bacardi to Pimms, we unscrewed the lot. After all, a little taste from each bottle would do no harm, would it? Who would notice? (The audience, that's who.)

By ten o'clock we were wasted and giggling like three school boys waiting to see the headmaster. We went on stage blown away. The audience were 'hurrah henrys' and upper class 'yuppies', sitting in lounge chairs, waiting to be entertained. They watched in bewilderment as we sang the wrong words to the wrong songs, did quick change impressions in the wrong costumes and basically had a three man party on stage. We were terrible and embarrassing. After ten minutes the first pint pot was thrown at us and then came beer mats, ashtrays and anything that was not screwed down. The manager told us to get off and said we wouldn't be getting our £60 fee. With words of wisdom and leadership from Steve – 'Let's get the fuck out of 'ere quick', we disembarked with the equipment down the pulleys and stairs to the van. Steve was collecting the glasses thrown at us and drinking the slops. The yuppies were now entertaining themselves and pissing in the pint pots. Steve was careful not to drink those.

We made a quick exit and started out on a four hour journey home with a bottle of cherry brandy that Steve had taken as credit for non-payment of our fee, the tea leaf. He slept all the way home cuddling his bottle. I wished he'd nicked whisky. I will never drink cherry brandy again. Never since have I been drunk before going on stage in over forty years. I have got drunk when on the stage but never before walking on!

Art, Bart & Fargo carried on for the next year then Richard decided a comedy musical show was not what he was looking for. He wanted to get into serious blues and rock music. Steve took a job at an off licence carrying out empty bottles. (Well, they were empty when he'd finished with them). As I was married, I still needed a proper job. After the band split up, I played in the local clubs at night and worked in a timber yard carrying wood by day. After they found out I had a criminal record for setting fields and houses on fire my contract was terminated. I then took a position at a local furniture store as a salesman, selling cheap furniture and carpets to people who couldn't afford them. They paid something like £2 a week for thirty years and this would furnish their house with rubbish settees, bedroom furniture and multi-coloured carpets until they died.

I didn't have the heart to take the customers' money and proceeded to make them laugh by doing Frank Spencer stunts like sliding down the shop stairs in a two seat sofa and swinging off the chandeliers as Quasimodo. I was earning more drumming at night and couldn't settle to selling beds. Most days I was asleep in them after arriving home from the clubs in the early hours of the morning. The customers thought this was a great novelty; me lying in a double divan in my pyjamas in the shop window, with a sign around my neck saying 30% off! Soon afterwards, I started at a brand new purpose built club called The Telstar in Bransholme, with three other excellent musicians. I was working five nights a week doing eight shows. The manager of the furniture shop moved the bed round the back so I could get a decent day's sleep.

Being young and totally irresponsible, I started having an affair with someone I fell in love with at The Telstar. Kathy was pregnant and was devastated when I left her. I had never in my life hurt anyone so badly before and at that time it ruined her life. Before our son Daniel was born, I briefly went back to Kathy but after a night at my old home I realised I had moved on and couldn't stay. We married far too young and I regret to this day the hurt and suffering I caused her. She went through a terrible time. However, she eventually married again, Daniel became her husband's son and she found the happiness she deserved. I married Lynda, the woman I met at the club, we have been together in a relationship for forty years and have two boys. This was the second beginning of my life and it led to another forty years full of ups and downs, traumas, hardship, some happiness and good times, some misery and pain that I caused the ones I love and those nearest to me. We have laughed and cried but we have survived to tell the tale.

For the second half of this book. I've got lots left to tell so if you're not bored, or can't sleep, then make some tea and read on. Otherwise, throw this book in the bin and read something from Richard & Judy! But if you still want to stay with me, I'll tell you more about my life. Joey, the drummer, the adventurer, the traveller, the entertainer – and always the comedian...

Here I am, all of nine months in my pram at the prefab in Cranbrook Avenue, Hull.

Me aged four in the garden at Cranbrook Avenue. I was in preparation for Le Tour de France. Which way to Brid?

Most of our holidays were spent at Bridlington. This is Mum and me at Wilsthorpe Camp near Bridlington sitting outside the ill-fated two bedroomed bungalow that Dad built.

Three years later and I'm training my younger sister Wendy in the art of tricycle racing at Sewerby Park, a stately home and gardens situated in a dramatic cliff-top position over looking Bridlington (of course!).

Just joined The French Foreign Legion. Waiting for the rest of my uniform to arrive!

Left: This was my fifth birthday party, and I was already surrounding myself with girls. I'm sitting on a stool my dad made.

Below: More in the garden at Cranbrook Avenue. Wendy and me, probably off to collect family allowance.

Here with Wendy, I'm playing the wooden guitar that Dad made for me. Eat your heart out Hank Marvin. I was nine.

Above: Wendy, Mum and me sitting on the harbour wall at Brid.

Left: I'm giving Wendy a lift 'cause we didn't have a car.

Mum, me and Wendy at Scarborough (makes a change from Bridlington!) doing my very first and utterly convincing impression of Charles Atlas.

Wendy, Mum and me sitting on the harbour wall at good old Brid.

A Family outing caught on the Box Brownie, guess where? (from left to right) Cousin Carol, Aunty Gladys, Mum, Sister Wendy, Aunty Moo, me, cousin Jeff, and cousin Alan.

Left: Me aged 16 with Mum Dad and Wendy at home (somebody should've said 'smile for the camera').

Right: Orchard Park School, 1965 and here I am waiting in line to accept my Duke of Edinburgh Bronze Award from Prince Philip with my pals in the Boys Brigade. I am the little one on the right. To think, I was once fourth in line to the throne.

Drumming up a storm for the American Troops in Germany before they go to war in Vietnam. (c.1970)

Richard Gabbitas who played lead guitar in The Losers Showband and me, c.1971. We'd just been stopped by the police they said, 'Pullover!'

Above Left: The Losers Showband publicity photo in Frankfurt Germany in 1971. (From left to right) me, John Bell (band leader, rhythm guitar and keyboards), Lesley Saxil-Neilsen (bass guitar), Richard Gabbitas (lead guitar) and Norma Grant (lead vocals).

Above right: Members of the Comedy Showband (left to right) Steve Wilkinson (bass), me (drums) and Richard Gabbitas (lead guitar) as Art, Bart and Fargo in 1973.

Above: Did I tell you we got married? Lynda and me outside Carolyn Place Register Office, August 23rd 1977.

Above left: Off to Scarborough on honeymoon. Came back the same night. Locked out of our hotel!

Left: Finally, Dutch Dash to Amsterdam, our first break together and where Lynda first found out I hid my money in a sock!

Kenny Barratt, Lynda and me, 'A rose between two thorns' in the comedy cabaret act called 'Pantomime' at Birkholme Country Club, Preston near Hull., 1979, and right: 'Go on, clap then!'

The Isle of Wight Days (1983):

Right: Entertaining at the Trevellyan Hotel Straight out of Burton's shop window.

Below: Our ad in the I.O.W. Tourist Board Brochure, 1983. It generated tons of business.

Mike Lodge, me and Johnny Pat doing The Andrews Sisters at B.P.
Sports and Social Club Saltend. (Circa 1989)

Above left: Inside Jojo's Cabaret Restaurant, Newport near Hull where I was at the same
time maître d', manager, waiter, barman, and comedian, no wonder I was sweating! (1988)

Above right: Mum's 70th Birthday at Jojo's 1993

The gang at Blazing Saddles 1994.
'Is that gun loaded'?
(Photo courtesy of HDM)

Ainsley and Howard. Comedy double act.   Right: Busking in a Bus shelter. (1995)

Above left: At Los Boliches, Fuengirola, Costa del Sol around 1999, here with Lynda sampling 'Talk of the Coast' as potential buyers.

Above right: Lynda.Thomsons Mediterranean working Cruise. Incognito!
'The Great Escape' in 2008.

Below: Norman Collier pedalling, Johnny Pat, Mike Lodge, and John Ainsley pushing me. 'The flat pack', just before leaving for Spain in February 2000. (Photo courtesy of HDM)

Above: Mike Lodge and me 'stocktaking' in Godshill Isle of Wight. A trip back in time, more than twenty years after we'd left Alverston Cottage. (2009)

Below: At John Ainsley's house. Norman Collier and Mike Lodge and me. 'Norman always kept us laughing'. (2012)

Top left: Joey and Simon 'looking for their pocket money'. (1982)

Top right: Son Simon, Lynda, me and son Joey.

Above: This photograph was requested by my mother-in-law Jean of all the men in her life on her 70th Birthday. Left to right. Robert, Richard John, Simon, Pete, Darren, me, Joey and Rodger.

Below: A family photograph. Kids, grandkids and in-laws all with my Dad. Back row, left to right; Joey, Richard, Wendy, Lynda, Jess, Ginny. Front row, left to right; Jono, Dad and me. (2004)

The (almost) unrecognisable me as Nurse Flossy in Snow White at The Theatre Royal Lincoln. (2018)

Spotted on my best selling DVD.

Performing at the 40th Anniversary of the Cromer Pier Summer Show in 2017

THE SECOND BEGINNING

Chapter 14

Telstar: All Cut and Dried

Lynda was working behind the bar at Telstar on an evening and was a hairdresser in the daytime. She was also a singer and worked with The Mecca big bands from the age of sixteen. She had sung in the clubs, both solo and in groups and at sixteen was in one of the first national girl group called Mandy and the Girlfriends in the early sixties. I left home and with no money, we lived for a week in the back room of the hairdressing shop she managed. The owner thought the world of Lynda and after drinking a bottle of sherry a day she would cut my blonde blue hair for free (that's what attracted hair to me).

Lynda was twenty seven and had a little boy of seven, Simon. He stayed at his gran's until Lynda's parents decided whether we were both responsible enough to give him a proper home. Lynda had her name on the council housing list and as fate had it, a flat in East Hull became available. We were very pleased as I was sick of sleeping under the driers and getting a bath in the shampoo basins at the hairdresser's. The flat was on the top floor of a tower block on Bilton Grange and unfurnished. The view from the eighth floor was superb. We were walking on eggshells at this time and could count proper friends on one hand, due to me leaving Kathy and setting up home with Lynda. Our parents were disgusted at what I'd done and we didn't feel good about ourselves. Kathy was in a very bad way and Lynda questioned the decisions I'd made. We were reminded of these every day with phone calls from people telling us how selfish we both were.

We both agreed to support Kathy financially and I virtually gave her all my wages. Lynda supported us with food and rent and paid the bills through her hairdressing job earnings. We were broke but with handouts and second hand furniture from friends and shop customers, Lynda made the flat very homely. She cooked lovely meals and with the £1.00 we had left I would visit the Bargain Booze shop and get a cheap bottle of plonk. (Steve was still working in there wringing out empty bottles.)

We both carried on working and I decided to bite the bullet and take the plunge as a solo comedian. I worked hard on an act and with Lynda's support, took to the stage in a black and white checked suit, with a bag full of props and some bookings from local agents. The fees were around £20 a night and if I worked three nights, £60 for the weekend was good money. My first show was on a Saturday night in Beverley at an Army NCO club. Lynda came with me and stood at the back door with it open for a quick getaway. I had done some of my sketches and impressions previously with the bands I'd worked with and knew that with the right audiences, this material worked. I walked on the stage with a pretence of confidence and the audience loved me. Success! Stardom here we come! I received nothing but praise. I was cock-a-hoop and full of myself. But this feeling only lasts with you until the next morning when the nerves and worry kick in again. The second show was on a Sunday at The Hawthorne club on Hessle Road. I was doing two shows, a noon and night. The lunchtime spot was full of men; mostly rugby players and dockers drinking twelve pints each before they went home for Sunday lunch and a kip.

I went on the stage and did my act for twenty minutes until the owner, ex-Hull FC and international rugby player, Johnny Whiteley, from the dressing room curtain, showed me a large stick with a hook on it and politely indicated, 'Get off or I'll pull you off.' John was getting bigger laughs than I was; I hadn't even had one small laugh. I retired to the dressing cupboard with the same feeling I would experience many times in the years ahead, those of complete humiliation and unworthiness. I was twenty four years of age, weighed 9 stone and still looked sixteen so trying to entertain 6'2" burly rugby players and fish dock workers who had experienced every hardship in life brought me back to earth. They didn't want a cabaret act, they wanted a blue comic to 'fuck and blind' and tell filthy gags. Johnny Whiteley was very understanding and knew this was only my second booking. He reluctantly let me perform to a mixed audience at night and I did better. Women felt sorry for this cheeky little lad doing impressions and comedy and some took me to their bosoms. This reminded me of my mother and being breastfed on those puppies at Townend Maternity Home when I was born.

I carried on and did the bookings I was offered. I wasn't happy because through lack of experience I either did well or died a death. The anxiety and stress at this point of my life was too much to cope with. I wasn't ready to be a solo comedian. The apprehension and worry of failure was too much for me. Then, new challenges presented themselves and Lynda and I joined the local Locarno and Mecca Band. This meant six nights a week which paid £100 a week for the two of us. With no stress of solo performances and clubland we went back to music with Lynda singing and me on drums. The band was a seven piece and here we were, with Lynda back again at Mecca's Tiffany's for the second time.

Now, as well as working until twelve at night, six nights a week, another opportunity came for us. Lynda's brother-in-law offered to set up Lynda and her sister in business with a small hairdressing shop. Could we cope? Could Lynda do two jobs? Should we try? Yes, we did. The shop was in Portobello Street, East Hull and with Lynda's experience in hairdressing, she would be the stylist and her sister would do the apprentice work. However, the partnership didn't flourish so we borrowed £1,300 from my parents and bought the brother-in-law out. Lynda went it alone.

One day, while I was outside on a ladder painting the fascia board of the shop, I saw Lynda working on her own, doing ten jobs at once. The shop was busy and what with the hairdressing and taking bookings on the phone she was near to tears. I couldn't bear see her like this so without a second thought I came down the ladder and started shampooing ladies in the sink. Now, apart from getting washed in the sink, this was a first for me and after doing four ladies, taking pins out, putting them under the drier, and answering the telephone I had discovered where my roots lay. (Not hairdressing.) I made the ladies laugh; they loved to come to the shop and be soaked in water as I shampooed them and towelled them down. I would get four driers full and then perform my cabaret act. This was easier than the clubs and they were paying for it. The shop was named All Cut & Dried (not many were dried) but Lynda was a good cutter. In fact, she was so good at cutting she once cut a lady's pearl necklace from around her neck. We scurried on the floor between the feet of the ladies under the driers, looking for pearls now covered in fluff and human hair. Happy days! We employed another hairdresser and Lynda carried on working day and night, cutting in the daytime and singing at night. Sometimes she got mixed up and cut hair on a night and sang in the daytime. We decided one would have to go and asked the other hairdresser to manage the shop to ease the stress of two jobs. This didn't work out as people missed the experience and quality Lynda had provided. We sold the shop with a pile of wet towels and a box full of bleached blue wigs thrown in. When you think of it, look at the experience I had achieved in ladies hairdressing. I had my hair dyed blue, drunk sherry with Lynda, slept under the driers, got bathed in the sink, drenched women while shampooing them and did my act while juggling pins and rollers. If Vidal Sassoon had seen me at work I could have made him a fortune. I was The Comedy Stylist!

The band was working every night but the bandleader was an alcoholic and sad to say, died at forty six years of age. We got another bandleader but the following Christmas he sacked me for fooling around on stage, making people laugh and not being able to count four in a bar. Well, on our breaks we would visit the pub across the road and I always counted more than four in the bar. Sometimes on a weekend there were a dozen at least.

We were still living in the Ivory Tower and I had to find another job. Lynda and I both left Mecca and I went to work in a man's boutique called Royce Manshop, a large retail business. The shop had three branches in the middle of Hull city centre and once again I entertained the general public whilst selling men's clothes. We had seven boys working in the shop; three of those lads were heterosexual and four were gay. The word gay for homosexuals had not been used yet. Gay then was to be happy and we were, laughing and messing about, trying on clothes, buying bacon sandwiches and sausage rolls and measuring men up for suits. I never did the inside leg – this was left to one of the four. My wages had dropped to £28 a week but if we reached our weekly targets and sold enough suits we got an extra £1 per sale plus a bit extra for an alteration. Some weeks I could make £40 and I was still playing drums in the evening I could earn £30 a week more. We were getting by.

Simon's gran had decided I wasn't a bad egg after all and let Simon visit the flat. He enjoyed coming to see his mum and together we built up a good relationship. Making everyone laugh seemed to be my purpose in life, apart from Lynda who I only made laugh when I gave her the housekeeping money. Somewhere along the line we had saved enough deposit for a house. We were both good managers. After all, Lynda had managed the hairdresser's and I'd managed myself, only spending £1 a week on a cheap bottle on wine. (Steve was still at Bargain Booze but now sat outside, begging for empty bottles)

We moved into a nice terraced house in a cul-de-sac off Holderness Road. We didn't have a removal van, we just threw the furniture off the eighth floor and what survived, did. When they say 'sticks of furniture,' that's what was left. We took our sticks and Lynda made us a lovely home. The bed was made from sticks, so was the settee and the kitchen table. We had a rockery in the garden and that attracted a stick insect. We had a walking stick and Lynda would hit me with it when I tried to make her laugh. She still has the stick under the bed after all these years. She never uses it now because I never make her laugh!

Around this time Lynda became pregnant and in January 1979 Joseph Samuel was born and Simon had a little brother. We were now a foursome. My mother and father had given in and accepted Lynda and our new family. Mum wanted to see her grandchild and offered to babysit. On a nightly basis we would drop little Joey off in the street and my mother would pick him up out of the gutter and feed him a warm rusk and homemade tomato soup. My father was still growing tomatoes and by now he couldn't get rid of them; they were pushing themselves out of the greenhouse door and down the garden path. You had to put wellingtons on to hang out the washing because your feet and ankles were covered in redskins and at the moment in time we had no Indians living near us. If you bought 8lb of Len's tomatoes you got a free chrysanthemum. He couldn't sell them either.

I still made people laugh so toyed with the idea of doing comedy again, this time forming a comedy musical singing trio. I bent Lynda's arm up her back and persuaded her to be in the act to provide the glamour needed. We auditioned a guitarist who could sing and loved comedy. We called ourselves Pantomime and that's what it was – a right pantomime! Our guitarist was called Kenny Barrett. He looked like Harpo Marx and had a small white van that we travelled around in. The van would only do sixty miles an hour and thirty uphill. If we were travelling to Sheffield for a Friday show we had to set off on a Wednesday to get there. Ken was methodical and kept everything from ropes, spare engine oil, props, wheel bearings, tool kits and a gear box in the van. Lynda had to sit in the front seat next to Ken while I sat on the roof rack next to his welding gear in case anything fell off the van.

The act was tight, we looked good and sang three part harmonies. Not together. Lynda would sing one part in the kitchen while I sang in the bathroom and Ken sang in the garage while jacking the van up. (That was the first sexual experience that van ever had.) We did comedy sketches, impressions and vocals and travelled around the country four or five nights a week, from Wales to Scotland in that little white van, chugging along like a small locomotive. It actually could have been a locomotive because Ken kept coal on the back seat.

I was building up confidence now as a comedy entertainer and gaining experience as the weeks and months went by. One night we were booked up into a social club in the North East. They were expecting a rock n roll band. We were a musical comedy cabaret act. I had applied black makeup to my face and done 'Sonny Boy' as Al Jolson – to a rock audience! The concert chairman was not pleased. After the first spot he came into the dressing room and expressed his feelings. 'Well, bonny lass', he said, 'yer a canny singer, and yous on the guitar are champion, but you in that fuckin' mask – yer crap!'

We toured nationally and abroad for two years before the pressure of leaving Joey with parents and friends became unacceptable. We did one tour abroad with him where he crawled on a snooker table and was picked up and looked after by a three girl act called The Mayer Sisters whilst we did our act. Another time in the North East he was in the dressing room crying at the side of the stage while we performed. He made so much noise and I felt so sorry for him, I wheeled him on the stage in his pushchair and a lady in the front row took him while we carried on. What a performance. The strain of grandparents looking after him got too much for all of us and Joey's asthma worsened. We had to make a decision. He was too tiny to bring into the act and could only scream. We needed someone who could sing. Could he juggle? Could he dance? Not yet. He could fill a nappy and throw milk bottles at the wall from his pram. Could I work this in the act? He could scream all night and only sleep three hours. He would spoil the act. Lynda decided to stay at home with him.

I looked at Ken, who looked at the van with its rear wheel now off, and saw a view of the road through the hole in the floor. Then and there I decided this would be the end of the longest running pantomime in history. We had done two years and sometimes I ran in front of the van and Lynda would shout, 'He's behind you.' (That was Ken driving with one hand and rolling a fag with the other) A real pantomime!

We honoured the bookings we had left and I decided to try it alone once again. I now had more experience and tested material. I was more used to the clubs and we had done nice cabaret work throughout the country. What could go wrong? Not being funny, that's what could go wrong. I looked a little older now – well, I was twenty seven but still looked eighteen. I took the bull by the horns and ventured out into the lion's den. I was David and the audience was Goliath. Slowly but surely, working every gig from pubs to clubs, holiday parks to theatres, I established myself as one of the worst comedians in the country. Money was good and I could earn £400 a week on a good run. I never did seaside summer shows because support acts in the theatre were paid little money and TV star comedians topping the bill never wanted support comedians to be funnier than they were. I earned three to four times more in the clubs so that's where I stayed for the next ten years. I missed opportunities for television and watched younger comedians pass me by. I worked solidly and hard, had no time for envy and was happy for the success that stardom brought them. It also brought some of them drugs, broken marriages and bankruptcy, not to mention the pressure of staying at the top with big earnings for as long as possible and sustaining the success of stardom. None of this affected me as my money never altered from £25 guineas in 1983 to 2016. I am grateful that I have earned a living making people laugh. We all have showbiz stories so here are one or two...

Chapter 15

The Ace of Clubs

I had been working for a couple of years throughout the country, staying in theatrical digs. When we had more than three day runs in the same area I would stay for whole weeks in the North East, Birmingham, Scotland and Wales. In the clubs, acts were usually booked for ten shows; nightly Monday to Saturday, then two on a Sunday, noon and night, usually with a stripper for the noon show.

The North East was the hardest area to entertain. From Middlesbrough, Stockton, Hartlepool then Sunderland, Jarrow, Newcastle and through the Tyne to Northumberland. The people there are kind and friendly but like Yorkshire folk, don't suffer fools gladly. As the Catherine Cookson films and novels showed, their working class upbringing meant they were hardworking people: miners, pitmen and ship builders. They had their own sense of humour but I think they kept this in a locked drawer because it was hard to penetrate. If they liked your act you were given the world. People would welcome you with open arms, take you home for Sunday lunch and eat you! Their sincerity and generosity was second to none.

Comedy is a personal thing and if a whole club of people didn't like you the majority of the time, you were paid off. That meant the concert chairman would give you half your money or a percentage of your money sometime in the evening and send you home. This could be in between songs, after your first spot. They didn't want your performance anymore. They were ruthless. If you were a singer, stripper, or worst of all, a comedian, you usually suffered the most. We dreaded travelling up there on a Sunday morning to face death (dying on your arse). The problem was they had seen and heard everything. The clubs were open seven nights a week, seven nights of entertainment. Some big clubs had three acts on a night with professional three piece bands working ten shows a week. Clubs had concert rooms and lounges that would hold three to five hundred people which were paid for by the breweries as long as the club exclusively sold their beer. This happened throughout the country. Newcastle Brewery in the North East, John Smith and Stones in Yorkshire, Marstons in the Midlands and Tartan and Methylated Spirits in Scotland. A drop of turps and a battered Mars Bar always went down a treat in Glasgow. It was a pity the English comedians didn't! The clubs were taking thousands of pounds per week, they had money in the bank and could borrow as much as they liked from the breweries. In some cases they had invested as much as £250,000 on refurbishing the venues. With clubs full and everyone working, miners and shipbuilders flocked there every night to play bingo, snooker and watch the entertainment. You couldn't believe clubs were full on a Monday night and that's where this next story begins.

I was booked at The Wallsend Social Club in the heart of shipbuilding in Newcastle (Sting wrote a stage play about it) There were three acts on and a three piece backing band. The club had recently been refurbished and was beautiful. They had a glass balcony upstairs around the perimeter of the club and aluminium tables and chairs graced the very expensive carpets in the concert room. It looked like a Habitat shop. I was the second act on and my fee was £80 for a forty five minute spot. After ten minutes of not being funny, some of the audience walked out. They did this in clubs if they didn't like you and would go to the next club down the street to see what act was on there, play the bingo and go for the full house. Being a martyr and a trouper and familiar with this situation I battled on and stayed on the stage for my forty five minutes. At the end of my performance nobody clapped. The concert chairman came up to me on the stage and put a wad of notes in front of me on the floor. I picked it up and counted it. With the microphone still on I said, 'There's only £20 here. I want my full money. I've done my time.' If you did your required spot they had to pay you in full. If they stopped your act because they didn't like you they paid you for how long you had performed. He replied ' You're crap, man, that's all you're worth, howay and shite' I understood, (not so much in Geordie terms), that this was all he was prepared to pay. 'I want my full money or I'm not leaving this stage,' I said. The room went deathly quiet; you could hear a pin drop (well, you wouldn't have heard it drop because of the thick new lush Axminster carpet) Now, I was threatening club procedure but then someone in the audience shouted, 'He is crap, man, but he's still entitled to his full money. He's done his time.' Then one or two more shouted, 'Yes, he's crap but get him off the stage so we can carry on with tonight's Housie Housie. It's £300 for a full house!' (Big money at that time.) The chairman stood looking at me then someone else piped up, 'Are you in the union, son?' They probably meant The Ship Builders and Welders, Steel Riveters and Clog Boot Union. I was in Equity, the Actors and Performers Union. 'Yes,' I replied. 'Then you want your full money,' he said. The audience responded, 'Aye, he does! ' The concert chairman took another £60 out of his pocket, gave me it and I walked off the stage to cheers and applause for my courage.

Another time, at the Middleton Social in Leeds the curtains were closed on me as the committee decided, 'He has to go.' A member of the audience stood up and took to the stage. Cheers from the audience filled the room for their greasy haired Elvis. He sung 'You ain't nothing but a hound dog' and they loved him. I walked into my dressing room and discreetly put away my suit, packed my props and quietly retreated through the back door(again). Acts always sussed out where the exit was. If there wasn't one you were fucked. That meant you had to face an audience who hated you, walk through the club audience and round the back to your waiting car that had probably had its tyres slashed.

Comments of 'Don't give up your day job,' would be jibed at you as well as 'When's the comedian coming on?' 'We've 'eard 'em all before.' I've had blokes in pubs walking past me and handing me their pints as they went for a piss. I've had drunks dancing to my gags. I've had beer mats and paper aeroplanes thrown at me, and that was only the audience.

Once, in Scotland, I set up my equipment and stage props in a village hall in a small hamlet outside of Edinburgh. Now this was not Wallsend Social Club but more like a Baptist church hall. Tables and chairs all set in a line and the smell of polish on the wooden shiny floor. I think it doubled as a schoolhouse in the daytime when the alcoholics (and there were plenty of them) used it from the evening onwards. I met the social convenor – that's what they called a concert secretary in Scotland. It was the afternoon and he offered me a double whiskey as soon as I arrived. I declined but he pushed up the optic for a double shot, one for himself and a double for me. 'Come on son, ye'll be having a drink'. I told him I didn't drink in the daytime and I was driving. This didn't worry him one bit as he drank both whiskies. I set the stage up with my array of props and hats from my props bag.

When I returned to the hall that evening the audience were all drinking whisky and pints and were in a jovial mood. On the stage were two musicians. I call them musicians; one sat on a chair behind a snare drum and the other played an accordion. Their music was a mixture of Jimmy Shand and Scottish marches from the Edinburgh tattoo! To make things worse, neither could read music and the drummer was wearing my Indian headdress I used in a sketch with my Tommy Cooper fez on the top. Now, there is unprofessional and totally unprofessional. This was the latter. I went mad at the drummer who saw no danger twiddling his drum sticks as the accordionist played 'Scotland the Brave'. I showed them the sheet music used for accompanying my singing and sketches and they looked at it in bewilderment. We decided they would busk what they could. The audience were drunkenly happy and luckily, accepted me and my comedy and laughed at everything, including the drummer who did his own comedy act behind my back.

In 1984 the National Miner's strike was on. In Jarrow, miners would hold their meetings in the clubs. They were on strike money but still drinking pints of beer at forty pence a pint and throwing the kids a bag of crisps for their dinners. Wives were outside too, manning soup kitchens, and riot police were working twenty four hour shifts, wage packets bulging. Arthur Scargill was attending three meetings a day up and down the country and whipping miners' enthusiasm to a frenzy, similar to a Third Reich rally. Could you believe that in this hostile fighting environment with picketing, scabs and family feuds, they still put on entertainment in the clubs in between meetings?

One Tuesday lunchtime they sent me to a club to entertain an audience, along with a stripper. She went on first after peeing in the dressing room sink in my presence then going on stage with her knickers in her hand to a slow handclap from the striking miners. I went on as the sound system was playing Chubby Brown comedy tapes in the background. Well, I'm cheeky but not blue and after chants from the audience of 'Fuck off!' I once again packed my comedy suit and props and hurried down the back stairs and joined the soup kitchen outside. With me only looking sixteen, I passed for a miner.

These were hard men who had hard jobs. They were fighting for their rights as their fathers and grandfathers had done over fifty years before them when the conditions in the pits were terrible. Men would come home covered in coal dust, their wives would take the tin baths off the hooks on back yard doors, fill them with water and scrub their husbands' backs. The men would then get out of the water and all the kids would get into the same black grime, then the wives would throw all the washing in the same water, followed by pots and pans. When this was done they would tip the water into the back yard and scrub the floor.

One Sunday evening in a club in Wakefield – or Rotherham or Sheffield (it doesn't really matter, the clubs were all the same) the weather was atrocious. Well, it was snowing atrociously with wind and sleet. I'd travelled over two hours in these conditions to get to this club.

Chapter 15: The Ace of Clubs

When I arrived, the atrocious snow was a foot thick in the car park. I skidded up the back fire escape, up two flights of wrought iron steps, carrying my equipment. I banged on the fire door and was let in. The whole procedure, getting in and setting up my equipment must have taken me ninety minutes. I arrived at 7 p.m. and by 8.45pm there were two people sitting in the concert room. I said to the concert chairman, 'Not many in tonight.' He replied, 'Would you come out on a night like this?' I performed to two men and a dog (the dog was the only one that smiled). It was an atrocious night!

Last but not least, I performed one Sunday lunchtime at a club in Yorkshire with a ventriloquist called Jack Beckett who had talking shoes. The soles of these shoes had faces and mouths; he put them on his hands and they talked. He had just finished a summer season at Blackpool with Ken Dodd. Good old fashioned variety. This was a family act and he was 'dying on his arse' in front of a male beer swilling Sunday lunch set of hairy arsed stokers! As his act got worse and worse the concert chairman spoke over his own microphone and said to Jack, ' No wonder they're not laughing , they can't hear the shoes – put the mike near the shoes.' Poor Jack walked off to his own footsteps, put the shoes in a dustbin and walked into the sea barefoot. He attempted the act once again in trainers but it didn't work. In fact, I don't think he ever worked his act again. The last I heard, he'd got a job in a shoe shop.

Am I painting a dark picture of show business? Yes! Well, some of the dressing rooms are bloody dark, especially when a fuse blows and no one knows where the fuse box is. I once worked on stage in the pitch dark for a full twenty minutes. That was at The Spa Theatre, Scarborough and the stage manager gathered a posse together to look for the electric cupboard. The audience lit cigarette lighters and we all sang war songs, just like during the blackouts in World War Two. Some of the audience put their handbags and programmes over their heads, knelt down and waited for the All Clear.

Joey Who?

The public see entertainers illuminated by stage lights, or in my case cigarette lighters, wearing sequinned stage clothes, perfectly made-up, with a smile wider than a fat girl wearing a thong! They sing, dance, juggle and perform as though their last breath depended on it. The audience don't know that you haven't spoken to the person standing next to you for the last five years. He sings flat, has bad breath, drinks too much, is always late, owes you £500 for half of the equipment. Some acts can also be smelly. I once worked with a three sister harmony act who wore the same underwear throughout a three week tour. They had to employ a stone mason as a roadie to separate them from their knickers every night!

The Roadies go to bookings with the artistes, are usually unemployed, carry equipment, smell and don't use deodorant. They all think they're Meatloaf and eat petrol station food; pies, crisps, kebabs and takeaways. They usually dress in black tee shirts and have a builder's crack looming out of the top of their baggy jeans. Their vocabulary on a microphone is limited to two words: 'One Two! One Two!' Usually, their claim to fame is they have worked with either The Who or Genesis and are in between world tours. So, at the moment, they welcome any work and are pleased to shag any of the audience who look upon them as superstars. They will drive the act's old transit van through the night for eight hour periods and live on a can of coke and a Yorkie bar. They usually don't get paid much, and own the one black tee shirt, two sizes too small that's never been washed, with a pungent aroma of beans coming from the armpits, with a mixture of diesel and curry sauce wiped on the front over the faded logo of Iron Maiden. They strut as they set up two speaker cabinets for a guitar vocal duo singing Abba's Greatest hits in a care home. That's a roadie!

Some acts are worse. I've seen white shirts with collars as black as a miner's neck and arm pits growing moss and smelling like the inside of a Turkish taxi driver's jock strap. The audience never witness these integral problems that the artistes incur, such as the snow and ice on a dark and slippery night, carrying equipment up back alley fire escapes in the dark; cold damp dressing rooms with ceilings dripping in condensation and brown cigarette tar; motorway diversions, roadworks, accidents and delays. All these leave you with only twenty minutes to arrive at the venue which is by now hostile and threatening you with non-payment unless you get your equipment and act ready in five minutes. When you do arrive, the shit hits the fan. Everybody is now sweating, looking for the nearest electric plug, moving equipment into the wrong position on the stage. Putting on those smelly stage clothes once again that have missed the promise of being washed one day. No time for a proper sound check, audience fidgeting because you're late and now the microphone with bad breath won't work, and oh yes, you need a wee – no sink so hold it! The stress and anxiety is overwhelming as you stand behind the club curtains which are held together by smoke and dust. You are announced to an audience sitting with bingo dobbers who are talking through your first spot and couldn't give a fuck. They are only waiting for the £10 flyer – a one line win on the bingo.

This was my introduction to show biz at the age of seventeen – and many more like me. This was my beginning in the northern clubs of the seventies and eighties. Every pop group thought they were The Beatles or The Shadows. Every male singer thought he was Cliff, Elvis, Johnny Mathis or PJ Proby. Every male singer had a special smelly suit on and every girl singer thought she was Patsy Cline, Dusty Springfield or Shirley Bassey. Nothing has changed, apart from the clubs where the audiences have nearly all disappeared and died. I died a few times myself but like Jesus, I was resurrected on the Sunday and worked a noon and night. At lunch time you would be graced with two lovely strippers or painters and decorators, depending on the size of their brush. They would perform before and after the comedian to an audience of beer swilling men who jeered, read newspapers and drank as many pints as possible before they went home to their wives for Sunday dinner. If the men accepted you were a 'decent turn' they would then bring their wives in the evening. The strippers and comedians were all heckled by the men. Once, in a Hull club I performed in, a stripper was so bad, they shouted 'pur 'em on!' In Jarrow, I walked on stage to "Fuck off! Fuck off!" to which I replied, 'I don't do requests." They still paid me off but many times I have left a club penniless, creeping out of the exit door in case somebody offered me ten pence!

We can all spot talent a mile away – or can we? Everybody knows what they like. It's a personal choice. All our tastes are different. Some people like Madonna. Some like Take That. Some like Lee Evans, some liked Tommy Cooper. Some like Gordon Ramsay! (I would rather watch Nigella Lawson licking chocolate off a wooden spoon)! You experience different tastes. All these people and many more; pop idols, comedians, chefs or Alan Titchmarshes have served their apprenticeships; years of moulding their craft, fine tuning their careers to stardom. Some of us have never made it! Like I said at the beginning, I have been close to stardom....

Chapter 16

Sun, Sea and Sand

In 1983 I travelled with Lynda to the Isle of Wight and worked there during the summer season in the holiday camps and hotels; a change from performing in awful clubs where bingo was the star billing. We would start in May and stay until September and take little Joey with us. I would work nine or ten shows a week. We rented several flats in those years and one year we stayed above the club where we were booked. We were on the job at the Whitecliffe Bay holiday Centre. The views across the Channel were stunning but the smell of chip fat and the noise from the club wafting upstairs twenty four hours a day put paid to this adventure so we moved to Shanklin and a large house converted into several flats. We loved the island and so in 1986, after three seasons, we decided to move there.

We bought Alverstone Cottage in Sandown, an eleven bedroom guesthouse. We had moved house three times in Hull and had made money on our property which we invested into the B &B business. Lynda was going to be responsible for the running of the business whilst I still did twelve shows a week. The place needed decorating but with Lynda's touch we made it homely and friendly and built a bar in the conservatory for the guests. It was horse work for £11 bed and breakfast and in those days we even did a three course evening meal with a choice. The guests loved our hospitality and would come to my shows after the evening meal, then drink in the bar until the early hours. There was laughter and frivolity and the till rang! It was a novelty, having a comedian as the barman, waiter, maid and bottle washer and people would tell their friends, 'Don't stay there – the place is a joke.' Apart from working all day and night it was another experience of life. I was a devil for punishment and should have learned the pitfalls of business. It's okay as an act you do for an hour to your audience then leave, whether they like it or not. Out of the back door. Finished. When you have a guest house or hotel the public are with you on demand twenty four hours a day. Most people are nice and respect your home. Others are shagging all night, grunting and groaning. Others get pissed and pee in the wardrobes. Some people sleep walk naked, up and down the hallway. (I had to apologise to the guests about that and promise I would never do it again) Old people leave skid marks on the sheets and pretend it's through eating chocolate in bed. People smoke in the rooms and some people leave without paying.

One afternoon about 4 p.m. a people carrier pulled up with and Indian Sikhs and his tribe inside. There were father, mother, grandma, granddad, aunties, uncles and children – and I spotted Ghandi driving! Little Joey said, 'Dad, there's someone banging on the front door with a beard.' I replied, 'No wonder I couldn't hear him.' We opened the door and the father said, 'Can we stay here'? I said, 'No problem' and brought them nine chairs to sit on the road. They asked for a special price for one night for nine people but they only wanted two rooms. We had a family room; two beds, two bunk beds and a twin with two single beds. That only made six beds. He said this would be okay. I thought two people would have to sleep standing up in the wardrobe or underneath the bed, or someone would have to kip with Grandma and Granddad. The house was empty so he haggled a price with me for two rooms and they moved in for the night. The women stayed in the rooms all evening while the men sat crossed legged in the lounge on our multi-coloured carpet and drank whisky. I thought one was going to fly off on it as he swept into the kitchen and asked if he could make tea in a saucepan for his party. He put the tea with water, sugar and milk all together – cold – in a saucepan and boiled the lot on our stove. They then drunk it in the lounge and retired to bed. In the morning they asked which way was Mecca as the driver who looked just like Ghandi was turning the van round. I pointed them towards the Locarno ballroom. I told him Lynda and I had been to Mecca many times and had played there in a band. I also told him my auntie used to play bingo there. He was very grateful for my knowledge and the whole party waved as they left, leaving two people in the wardrobe and one under the bed. The father was an Indian surgeon and had removed a member of his party's boil on their backside during the night. He was from Bengal and we later found out he was a Bengal Lancer!

We promoted Alverstone Cottage with a comedy appeal to guests who had a sense of humour. We advertised with the Isle of Wight Tourist Board in their Hotels Brochure. Lynda, little Joey and I dressed up in Edwardian costume and sold the holiday with items such as * ONLY 35 MILES FROM THE BEACH* * WE LOVE CHILDREN BUT CANNOT EAT A FULL ONE * * SEE THE STARS AT NIGHT THROUGH THE HOLE IN YOUR BEDROOM CEILING* RUNNING WATER IN EVERY ROOM FROM THE SEWER PIPE NEXT DOOR * *SLEEP IN TILL 12 NOON THEN MAKE THE BEDS YOURSELF * It worked a treat but we were nearly banned from the English Tourist Board for ridiculing our industry. However, when we were inspected and the stars given out for accommodation we were awarded a bronze star and the teacher said, 'Could do better'. We did – with our next advert.

Then we became more outrageous and greeted guests as Manuel and Basil Fawlty. Simon had now arrived to live with us. He was nineteen by then and his Gran wanted rid of him because of the mess in his bedroom. He played a big part in the running of the business as a waiter, cook and barmen and experienced working with the general public at first hand. We threw him in the deep end. He played Manuel and I was Basil. We insulted guests when they arrived, gave them the wrong food in the dining room, put them in the wrong rooms and generally took the piss. 75% of visitors accepted the good fun and humour because they had booked in good spirit. 25% didn't understand what was going on and booked themselves into Parkhurst for the night

– they felt safer inside four prison walls. Despite all the fun and tomfoolery our standards were high, the beds were clean, our food was good and we offered a choice: Like it or Leave it. Everyone liked it.

However, another recession came in the nineties and hit us once again. Business became poor; hotels went into receivership and were repossessed by the banks. Properties were turned into care and nursing homes and the English holiday market and resorts went into decline. Some hoteliers were in so much debt to the banks they foreclosed and sold their businesses for next to nothing, leaving the hoteliers penniless and homeless. I know of two good friends who ended up in sheltered accommodation. Luck was with us somehow and we sold Alverstone Cottage for double what we paid for it.

In the meantime, I had been back home, gigging up North in the clubs through the week to pay the bills and had spotted a Greek restaurant, The Attica, for sale on the outskirts of Hull, in Newport. It was going cheap because the owner kept budgies in a cage. The place was run down and I asked Lynda if we should buy it and turn it into JOJO's, a cabaret restaurant. To this day I can't believe she agreed to what would be nine years of total commitment, nonstop work, slavery and hell. You see, clubland was suffering by then and I was always trying to think ahead, always planning for the future, always looking at new business prospects. I have never learned and to this day I am always chasing rainbows. I realised I would never make the big time as a TV star comedian but would, and always have, made a good living from show business. In my profession you never know where the next penny is coming from and it always worried me and caused anxiety and stress. If I had a future plan to go alongside my work as a comedian then I was happy. The trouble was I always involved other people to make things happen and that didn't make Lynda happy!

Chapter 17

Jojo's and Blazing Saddles

In 1988 we moved from the Isle of Wight and into the Attica Greek restaurant with the accommodation above. We painted and decorated, scrubbed and cleaned, got rid of all the smashed plates, and bought some new tables and chairs. We put on an English menu and Lynda was cooking once again, with the help of her mum and two other ladies in the kitchen. We hired waitresses and bar staff and advertised: 'A three course meal with Comedy Cabaret JOEY HOWARD.' The country was depressed, people were depressed and money was tight (especially in Yorkshire – where it's always been tight.) This was something different – food and cabaret. We could seat ninety people and in the first weekend, by advertising, we filled it. Newport which was fifteen miles from nowhere but I knew if we could get bums on seats people would come – and they did. We changed the name to Jojo's and the bookings started to come in because we were different. After the meal they enjoyed my show and then danced to Simon's disco. Yes, by now Simon was twenty and a toilet cleaner, barman, chef, painter and decorator, pipe cleaner and DJ. I trained him well and paid him in crisps and coke with twenty Benson & Hedges thrown in on a weekend because he had now started to smoke. Many a night I had to throw a bucket of water over him when he set himself on fire. Lynda, when she'd finished cooking, came out to sing from the kitchen and we had a live three piece band as well. Little Joey was growing up fast too. He was ten by then and his school uniform was too small. He was still in the khaki white shorts, white socks and Clarks sandals I'd given him from my childhood. He looked like one of the Von Trapp family. So I dipped into my piggy bank under the bed and bought him a pink vest and plastic trousers. He also had a pin put through his nose to match his

115

pink hair. He went off like that, never to be seen again, apart from as Po, going up and down on television at a Sid Vicious concert.

At Jojo's I would meet and greet people in black tie and tuxedo; (no trousers, just black tie and tuxedo). This went down well as I took the table orders, served drinks from behind the bar, changed barrels, served the wine and put the drunks back on the coaches and in the taxis. At 10.00 pm I would then change into Mr Show Business and perform my one hour comedy show. Birthday parties, hen nights, weddings, retirement functions, Christmas nights – we did the lot.

Now I had finished doing the clubs I concentrated all my time and money on Jojo's. We were turning bookings away; the place wasn't big enough and we needed more space. The house next door was up for sale so we bought it with money I had in a small tin box under the bed. We obtained a mortgage and bought Binbrook House to enhance the business. We decorated, painted scrubbed, knocked a wall out and made it bigger. We carried on working very hard for another year then a building project manager told me that for £60,000 he could make it even bigger by knocking walls and the ceiling out. Then we could have a balcony that went around the inside of the building. This would make room for a staircase up to the top floor where we could seat another thirty people. The place was going to be themed like an Italian courtyard. We would have false doors and windows and canopies around the building, making the inside look like shop fronts and houses with a courtyard in the middle for seating. The upstairs would be decorated the same. It was painted in Mediterranean colours and looked like a film set. New tables and chairs were bought and a brand new kitchen with a walk in freezer was installed. The project building manager said he could refurbish and complete it all in six weeks. A complete new look.

After two weeks we saw men arrive as pubs were emptied on the east side of Hull and labourers gathered to work on this project. If you can imagine the crew from the Bounty with earrings, tattoos, bent noses and legs missing, patches over one eye, pistols and cutlasses. This was what turned up. A motley crew of out of work scavengers who came in an open top lorry. They knocked down the walls by firing a cannon and swinging from wall to wall as if boarding a ship on a raiding party. Through the night they were on double time wages to get the job finished. I would lie in bed listening to, hopefully, men working but all I could hear was snoring and the rustling of cards being dealt as they played poker. After three weeks no progress was being made but when I consulted the project manager he assured me everything was in hand. The only thing I could see in hand was the pint tea mugs being brewed all day by this posse of cowboys. I decided to help myself and donned a hard hat and got stuck in with labouring. This didn't go down well with the cowboys and a gun fight started at the Ok Corral. I told them and the projects manager if progress wasn't made now, in the last three weeks they wouldn't get paid. The manager walked off the job and went on holiday to Tenerife and half the work force never turned up again.

The men that were left worked hard for me and eventually, on the last week, we could see some light – through the hole in the ceiling not yet finished. Because of the balcony upstairs we should have had a fire escape fitted and drawn up in the plans. This was omitted from the drawings and upon inspection of the building a fire officer said we couldn't open in a week's time without a fire escape. I asked several companies but in only a week, nobody could make me a wrought iron fire escape coming from the top of the building and down the exterior of the back wall. We were also approaching a bank holiday and in a four day week, nobody was interested. One firm said they could make it in two weeks and it would cost £16.000. We had bookings for the opening night that I had to cancel and also find another £16.000 to finish the job. However, the cowboys who were left with me robbed a stagecoach travelling from Hull to Beverley and blew the safe from the back of a Lloyds Bank back wall with the cannon used for knocking walls through. We opened two weeks later. If only the public knew what we had been through to get open. 'Never again,' we said. (Read on!)

The new Jojo's was a tremendous success and for the next five years we did well. We changed the Binbrook room into an a la carte restaurant as an addition to the cabaret dining and Lynda presented a gourmet menu for discerning diners who wanted the luxury of excellent food served in an intimate setting. We organised a local coach company that brought parties from Hull and East Yorkshire for the cabaret dining with an all-inclusive price for travel, a show and a meal. Some nights the coach was held up by the cowboys we had sacked off the job and as well as the coach driver, we employed a sheriff and deputy to ride shotgun. The weekends were busy and we were serving a hundred and fifty people in two hours. There were six staff in the kitchen and fifteen serving the tables and behind the bar. This was a weekend venue and midweek was quiet so we had the idea of putting on ladies' nights with supper and a male stripper. Now this brought in extra revenue but also involved ladies having sex in the dressing rooms and getting the full Monty from these male artistes who were very well endowed. You wouldn't believe what went on upstairs. I even found a stripper having sex with two women in our private bathroom – in the bath! All this for the price of chicken and chips and some women upstairs had a sausage thrown in. This had to stop as no one had invited me to join in. Men booked the venue for private parties, also with female strippers, and after witnessing sex on the dance floor and men standing in line to take part I decided this couldn't carry on. It was embarrassing and tasteless and nobody ate the food!

After the seven year itch (and there was a lot of itching after shagging the strippers) trade became less and less. You are only flavour of the month for a certain length of time and sorry to say, our time was up. We still owed money on the building and needed to carry on 'What now?' I asked myself. Lynda never asked – she just wanted a quiet life but I'm afraid this wasn't to be. After consulting my tarot cards I thought the business could be rescued so we changed Jojo's into 'Blazing Saddles', a Wild West Restaurant serving burgers, ribs, big steaks and Line dancing. (If only I had consulted the cowboys.)

I borrowed another £30,000 from the bank and we changed the place into a Wild West saloon. It looked fabulous and we even had a wagon on the stage with a honky-tonk piano in the back for shows. We dressed as cowboys (the labourers from Jojo's sold us their clothes and guns) – and off we went again! With new branding and a piano player on the wagon (well, he liked a drink) out came the burgers, corn on the cob, T bone steaks and barbeque ribs. With a fabulous write-up in the local papers and The Yorkshire Post we once again went into battle. On the first day of opening over a hundred and fifty people turned up to see what the fuss was all about. It was sheer hell. The kitchen couldn't cope with the numbers and the service wasn't good enough so our reputation suffered. Although we tried serving smaller tables and parties who loved the environment and the theme, it never took off. I was line dancing alone and the piano player shot himself. Well, somebody from the kitchen shot him first for repeating the same tunes every half an hour. I brought in country and western artists to see if that would work but they were so bad 'the dog on the porch' died several times!

I had tried something that if placed in Disney World would have taken off. If it had been on the coast it would probably have taken off too. Fifteen miles between Hull and Goole, it didn't take off. Theme restaurants or pubs only last maybe three years – ours didn't last twelve months. With my Winchester rifle I decided to walk into the car park and shoot myself but Lynda said, 'Don't do it! Don't leave me with this debt!'

I went to the bank again and they rounded up the horses in the corral and put jockeys on them at Beverley races. Not one a winner so they wanted their money back. By now I owed them £90,000. They closed the business and sold it to a builder for £60,000. He built four small detached houses on the front and four large four bedroom houses on the car park and made £1,000.000! For all our efforts, somebody else won the lottery – again! Fortunately, we had bought a small house across the road from the restaurant that the bank grudgingly allowed us to keep, so at least we had somewhere to live.

During our time at Blazing Saddles we formed a country band and topped the bill at our own venue. I played drums, Lynda sang; we had Ken Wright on guitar, Don Hanson on bass and Pete Green (my brother-in-law) played second guitar. We called ourselves Lyn. C. Doyle and the Loan Arrangers. Along with Lynda, each of us had a pseudonym to aid publicity and hopefully, to achieve notoriety for the band. I was Bill Ding Ashed, Ken was Rusty Strings; Don was Tex Drugs and Pete was Chester Drawers.

When Blazing Saddles went into decline in 1994 and was in receivership, the band went on the road for a year to earn some money to live. We became quite popular and were invited to perform at several well established country conventions. The country critics rated us highly in their regional country magazines. But – 'thar ain't no gold in them thar hills' – not when it's a five-way split, so Lyn. C. Doyle and the Loan Arrangers was disbanded on New Year's Eve 1994. Then, enter John Ainsley....

Chapter 18

Ainsley and Howard

People of all walks of life came to Jojo's over the years and a man who is still my good friend to this day, John Ainsley, brought his father-in-law, Norman Collier to see my show. Norman was one of Britain's most celebrated and talented TV comedians. He worked nationally and was a great favourite of thousands of people who loved his mad cap humour. In the seventies he performed in every club, theatre and cabaret venue, as well as appearing at The London Palladium. I was honoured and privileged to see him at our venue and he and John cried through my comedy act. (I wanted them to laugh but tears were running down their faces). It was a compliment and Norman, John and I became very close friends until Norman passed away in 2014.

John Ainsley had my sense of humour and was a very funny man. He was a gifted impressionist and observer of people and could mimic anybody you could care to mention, from friends and colleagues to politicians and celebrities. He had a business selling second hand cars in the daytime but did the clubs at weekends, performing in a singing comedy duo. He wanted more out of show business but didn't want to be a solo comedian. He was talented enough but needed the support and guidance of a partner. There would have been no Morecambe and Wise without Eric Morecambe; no Cannon & Ball without Bobby Ball; no Little & Large without Eddie and no Rod Hull without Emu.

John had some good contacts in business so together we rehearsed a routine and in 1995 we launched a comedy act that would pay us in pennies and coppers for the next two years. We were called Ainsley and Howard and we played in pubs, clubs and theatres, did corporate functions, made some comedy films for advertising companies and did a television warm up slot for a quiz show. I also ironed his socks and

121

underpants when we worked away.

I came on the stage alone and sang my introductory song. This has always broken the ice between artist and audience. If you can sing an opening song, at least the punters can see you have a modest degree of talent before you die on your arse trying to be funny. I would then (as I still do now) welcome the audience into this 'humble abode' or 'this disused Co-operative funeral hall' or '1958 Scout hut'. After winning them over with my riveting personality and comedy wit, I would explain that I had just returned from the Costa Del Sol, working in the sun as a pedalo attendant on the beach and picking up lobsters from the posh girls. I'd say I was so excited to be in this arena of entertainment, loved by an audience who were queuing for bingo tickets and dobbers. After twenty minutes of this merriment, John would come through the audience dressed in a flat cap, dirty old jacket, tie and shirt with trousers to match, looking basically like one of the men from the committee. (In fact, he was better dressed than most of the men on the committee.) John kept these clothes in a holdall and without a word of a lie, never washed or changed them in two years. He was a bit like John Bell from the Losers; his stage clothes hummed a tune of their own. John was a clean person in his civvies but with a sweat on, working on stage, he smelt like a wet dog in a caravan.

John got very nervous before performing and went as pale as a sheet. He smoked ten cigs and drank two or three bottles of beer or cider to calm himself down. (I always picked the old soaks didn't I?) But when he went on that stage he flourished and blossomed like a flower, using his superb clowning skills to portray all his different characters. In later years, John was a big success at business meetings in the car industry and housing market, doing impressions of highly influential guests and bringing his audiences to their knees while he virtually just took the mickey.

John would stagger through the audience, acting drunk and singing out of key, to the surprise of the punters, then join me on stage. Now, because he came from the back of the room, most times he was not seen by the audience as he'd often change in the car or men's toilets. He was never challenged or accosted in the toilets because in his stage clothes he smelt like a toilet and if the door was closed no one would want to engage with the smell coming from under the door. This was a safe haven for John. The act then continued with me telling the audience I could do hypnosis and put anyone to sleep. John would comment that the audience were already asleep after I had sung. Then he'd bet me I couldn't put him in a trance. We would go through comic movements of applying hypnotic spells before he dropped his head in a sleep. I would then ask the audience, 'What would you like me to do with him?' Some people shouted, 'Give him a bath!' Others said, 'Make the act funny.' This, I knew was impossible. I would make John do animal impressions and when I brought him out of his sleep he would take on the role of a chicken, a pig, a sheep or a monkey. If the audience was laughing by now we had them; if they weren't laughing, they were standing waiting for bingo tickets. We would then do several routines of impressions and sketches while John was under hypnosis. The act was polished, clean and funny and audiences laughed. One of our successes (and there was only was one) was when we travelled abroad for Thomson's holidays on tours in Spain, Greece and Italy. We worked to English holiday makers in Thomson's resorts and spent six months in the summer travelling from English airports to destinations you only dreamed of. Thomson's holiday hotels were everywhere throughout Europe and we worked outside near the swimming pools, to courtyards and apartments full of holidaymakers. There was an outside stage, lighting and pa system. The cabaret was always performed outside during the summer because of the heat. If the act was bad the audience could have a quick getaway, as well as throwing the comedians and entertainers in the pool. It was like doing Woodstock to 300 people. In Gibraltar the monkeys would come down off the rock and nick your act. I often saw two monkeys in the street putting each other to sleep, one bearing his red bottom to the other one. They got bigger laughs than John and I did. Maybe John should have bared his pink bottom whilst eating a banana. That would have got a laugh!

The temperature on some nights was 40 degrees. Can you imagine the heat coming off John's coat and body? The men in the audience were in shorts, short sleeved shirts, the women in cotton dresses. John Ainsley was dressed in an old tweed jacket covered in green mould and moss, a shirt that a tramp would have given away and trousers that would have won first prize at Brand's Hatch (Yes, you've guessed – plenty of skids!) People thought he was on fire as the steam left his body and water vapour collected in the turn-ups of his woollen grey trousers. When we had finished the act and John took a wet flannel to his steaming body as flies would gulp for air, trying to find a way out of the suitcase he put his clothes in. When going home through customs John never had an address label on his luggage. Instead, he had a skull and crossbones marked 'Poisonous'. I've laughed with John over the years about these clothes and when we finished the act they were sent to Oxfam to put on the 50 pence rail.

We travelled on over thirty flights that summer, sometimes doing three to four flights a day and only making each flight by minutes. Our schedule was hectic and for one performance our props and drums which were used in the act only arrived (with John's smelly suitcase) minutes before the act had finished. We got by and ad-libbed our way through our performance by selling postcards of Menorca and Majorca to the audience and blowing balloons up for the kids. When the shows had finished we would mingle with the audience at the bar for free drinks and John would make them laugh showing them his bank statements. We had a budget to live off of £13 a day that was inclusive of food and drink, deodorant and soap. After work in the wee small hours of the morning we would visit bars and cafes and sell the postcards to holidaymakers and swim in the sea so John could save money on soap.

Chapter 18: Ainsley and Howard

One night I stayed in the apartment and John went out alone, drinking. After visiting some local bars and sampling many San Miguels, he decided to go for a walk on the beach. It was a full moon; the sea was calm and shone like black oil over the bay. Being a naturist and wanting to shed his stage clothes he stripped off naked and walked into the water, thinking in a drunken stupor he could swim home. Now, anybody in their right mind would have realised this was probably a three thousand mile event. Considering John had only got his 3rd class swimming certificate for three lengths of breast stroke at the local baths, this was no mean task. However, always looking for adventure and a challenge, he got his hair wet and plunged into the murky depths of the Mediterranean. After a minute, though, he changed his mind and turned around for the shore only to see a large black labrador sitting watching him on the beach. The dog was growling, its tongue was out, its jaws were dripping with saliva and its eyes were red as though possessed by the antichrist.

As John was about to come out of the water holding his private parts so as not to encourage the dog into sexual harassment, he clenched his bits and walked a little way in the water. The dog growled and followed him so John then slowly walked back into the water and started to swim further down the beach. But the moon was shining and the dog could see John's movements. John swam another thirty yards and now with seaweed hanging from his tackle, waded once again out of the sea. But the dog had followed him and was still there, growling and licking his lips. John stood for another half an hour until the dog disappeared. Now to be honest, I'd seen John naked and wouldn't have eaten him myself unless I was very hungry! John stood in the water waist high with things starting to shrivel. By that time, he'd made another friend as a jelly fish had attached its self to his bollocks and was eating the seaweed. At least someone was having a meal' As John swam back down the beach and found his clothes in a little pile, he put them on over his wet body then someone came along and asked him, "Have you seen my dog?" He walked back to the apartment, stripped off, and hung his wet clothes on the balcony, still shivering but sober by now. He wrapped himself in a blanket and only cheered up when I laughed hysterically at his story!

In the winter, back in England, we worked consistently, with John doing two jobs, keeping his garage going and indulging himself in show business. We worked all over the country and collected comedy awards in Blackpool and the Midlands. We also travelled to South Wales, as many acts did. Welsh audiences loved entertainment and comedy and clubland was always busy. I loved Wales because I'd seen 'Zulu'!

Ainsley & Howard carried on working, winning awards and accolades, with good reviews throughout the country until 1997. However, John was trying to run his garage as well as travelling with the duo and was slowly burning himself out, working day and night. The garage was suffering financially and although he loved what we were doing something had to give. John was married with three kids and living on £13 a day for booze and fags he was struggling. We only got a little more money between us than a solo comedian did.

One day at the airport after talking to his accountant, he sat with his head in his hands and told me he couldn't carry on with the act. We honoured the bookings we had then John went back to work as Arthur Daley, selling second hand motors .He kept his stage clothes and wore them at work to clean and repair cars. My career once again was undecided but with the bones from the act, I adapted the material and put the audience to sleep by myself. I dropped the hypnotism and condensed the stand-up and comedy sketches into THE JOEY HOWARD ONE MAN SHOW.

I missed John at first but after tweaking and developing my own personality I gradually started to feel comfortable and confident alone on stage and started to gain success again. The act consisted of twenty to forty minutes stand-up then I would go into my props and do comedy routines and sketches, basically from Ainsley & Howard. At the end of the routine I would do a drum feature and play on tables, chairs and glasses. This always went well and would get me out of the shit if the comedy didn't work. Eventually, the whole show would last twenty minutes to two hours, depending on laughter, crying and looking for a back door. My work was getting better and I started performing for the holiday companies such as Pontin's, Warner's and Thomson's abroad. After doing well nationwide I was now paying myself £26 a day – double the Ainsley & Howard money. My earnings were good and I was doing around six shows per week but travelling 1500 miles to do them. That's 80,000 miles per year – a lot of diesel, car tyres and engines. The cruise ships were becoming popular and more accessible to the working man and comedy was a part of their new entertainment programmes. So I took a chance – and went cruising!

Chapter 19

Cruising

Since the 1900's cruising had been popular with the English and aristocracy and Cunard ruled the waves when it came to passenger liners. Companies such as Ellerman Wilson Line from Hull shipped cargo and passengers together all around the world. (What a squeeze all together in one bloody cabin!) In those days there were first class and third class passengers. Third class had a swimming certificate but they were not allowed in the life boats and had to fend for themselves. First class were allowed in the life boats only if there were enough seats and they had a big fat cheque book. The Titanic went down because too many passengers put ice in their drinks and it tipped up at one side. Other people jumped overboard because they couldn't listen to the band playing any longer. When we were little, if anyone you knew had been on a cruise, they were either very posh or had won the pools. Twenty years ago when the recession bit once again for the second time, decisions had to be made in the holiday market to keep hotels, holiday parks and cruise ships ticking over and afloat. The ships cut their cloth accordingly and offered reasonable prices for the working man to travel around the world in his Clark's sandals, grey socks and multi-coloured Hawaiian shirt. This was a fabulous alternative to the Costa del Sol and Benidorm, although most cruise ships would visit those places and drop off these passengers to buy more Hawaiian shirts and cheap trainers, then pull up the gang plank, hopefully never to see them again, apart from floating on a raft up the channel.

I have been on world cruises as a comedian and once travelled twenty six hours from Heathrow to Bangkok on an aeroplane without hardly moving from my seat. I watched the same film on the back of the seat in front four times. I then flew another eight hours to Adelaide in Australia before meeting the ship in Perth and carrying on throughout the globe. On world cruises guests pay as much as £20.000 – £30.000 for seventeen weeks at sea. (I told them the Isle of Wight ferry was only £60) They have a penthouse suite, black tie dinner every night and a twenty four hour butler service. Nowadays you can go with Thomson's for £599 for the week and sit in the cabin in your underpants and Hawaiian shirt whilst the cabin steward pokes a slice of toast under your door as an alternative. The cabin stewards on all ships are excellent and usually Filipino by race. I had a very friendly steward on one cruise. The first evening he made my white towel into a swan and placed it on my pillow. The second evening he placed a red rose on my pillow. The third evening he placed a chocolate on my pillow. The fourth evening he placed his pyjamas on my pillow (how friendly was that?) After a week you are expected to give your steward a tip. I told him to remove the soap out of the shower tray in case I slipped!

I've met bank managers, surgeons, policemen, judges, university lecturers, traffic wardens, school cleaners and a lollipop lady – all looking for the same thing, to get off the ship when it's in a force nine gale. From all walks of life they hand over their well-earned cash and say 'Entertain me, feed me, take me on day trips to exotic locations costing £100 each.' This does include a cheese sandwich because the Brits will not try any foreign muck or venture down a back street for a taste of culture when there's the ship's buffet on board and served every day at 12.30 p.m. You see, they've paid for that and know what they're eating. Passengers love to be together all day and all night, eating together, playing the ship's games together, playing cards together, dancing together, and in some cases, with single passengers, sleeping together! Well, why not if you're single? What's wrong if you're in your seventies and once again coming before the mast? They go on trips together and walk around foreign towns and cities, herded together by the cruise director. If you get a full coach together at £100 per person with fifty people on board that's worth £5,000, a nice earner for the ship; a good profit considering they have only taken you three miles up a Greek mountain to watch a shepherd boy herd a flock of goats together and blow his horn whilst his grandmother sits on a step and curdles smelly cheese. Passengers love it as long as they're together, don't have to speak Greek and can point at foreigners with their finger and shout, 'Do you know where we can get a cup of tea?' English people always think foreigners are deaf so they shout loud and do signing at them. Of course, most foreigners don't drink twelve gallons of tea a day so the English have to go back to the ship at 12.30 p.m. for tea in a tea pot and another three course meal.

On cruises, people can eat all day long and usually do. They gain weight on average a stone a week. After seventeen weeks, the passengers on world cruises have to be airlifted off the ship at Southampton on a crane and all their clothes sent to the British Red Cross because they'll never fit them again. There are keep fit classes on board and the gym is usually on the thirteenth deck. Passengers now weighing twenty three stone, after puffing and blowing and out of breath, can't make the steps to the gym and stop off on deck twelve for another afternoon of cakes, scones and 'a nice cup of tea'. The equipment in the gyms is in excellent condition because it is never used. If you need to find solace on a ship go to the gym; you can be on your own for hours unless you see a twenty three stone pensioner on a rowing machine eating a scone.

You can eat six meals a day on a cruise and in between those meals the staff walk around the decks wiping passengers' faces with warm sponges. Breakfasts are delicious, with full continental including all the hams and cheeses and different fruits and yogurts in their plenty. You can have American pancakes and kippers and smoked salmon (Americans like such as that with bacon). You can have a full English and strawberries to follow. You can even have a boiled egg with Marmite soldiers if you're not hungry. All this is cleared away and then 'elevenses' appear. This consists of small sandwiches, petit fours and cakes with biscuits and 'a nice cup of tea'. This is all cleared away and then at 1.00 pm out comes the buffet, carvery and everything the chef puts together that was left from yesterday. The choices are fabulous, with everything from curries to fish and different dishes from around the world.

All this is then cleared away but not before the coach has returned with fifty people wanting feeding and not wanting to try 'that foreign muck', and the need for another gallon of English tea. This is all cleared away. At 3.30 p.m. they set up again for high tea and usually, this can be taken in the ship's lounges or cabaret rooms or sneaked into the gym. This usually consists of all the cakes and biscuits and petit fours that were brought out at elevenses and after breakfast that nobody could face. I do tell a lie – I have had on the side of my tea cup saucer a half nibbled digestive that some fat twat attempted to eat, changed his mind and put back. At 5.00 pm this is all put away again, and then the restaurants open at 7.00 p.m.

This is for formal dinner where the tables are usually set for eight people on a circular table. Men are in black tie and women in evening dresses that they change every night for fear that the ladies on the opposite table might see them in the same bloody dress twice. They spend two hours telling each other how many cruises they've been on and how much wealth they have. Then the next night they engage in the same conversation with a different eight guests until they reach the captain's table and bullshit him. 'How marvellous you are steering the ship whilst sitting in the restaurant having dinner with us!' The Captain smiles and he tells them the same tales of the sea every night. They can't get enough of his stories, hang onto his every word and laugh at his jokes. They have their picture taken with him and he signs autographs. 'I hope I'll go down as well as he does,' I think. I am kidding myself; after all, I don't wear a uniform, stand on the bridge looking at women passengers in bikinis through binoculars and blow down a brass tube in the engine room. (I saw Titanic. It's always a big hit in the ship's cinema.) Passengers put their lives in the captain's hands. I looked at his hands – he could only get one passenger in each palm. A captain can also marry people at sea. I once saw a man chaining himself to the ship's railings because he didn't want to get married at sea or any other place. He was taken to his cabin where his Filipino cabin steward made him a swan towel and gave him a chocolate and a rose from his pillow. They put on the pyjamas together and are now living happily in Bangkok. After the Captain has done his nightly act and everyone has eaten the nine courses, the chefs and kitchen staff are presented to the tables to show how marvellous their food was. Male passengers then go to the toilets for a fart and a burp and the women retire to the ladies' powder room, lift up their evening dresses to tinkle. Everything is cleared away – again.

In 2008 I went cruising alone as Lynda was working in Ann Summers selling large luminous yellow condoms to Chinese tourists. She later quit as she couldn't get batteries for her toys. Instead, she got herself a window cleaning round with a brand new bucket, wash leather and ladder. She was very popular doing outside top bedroom windows and had a lot of men holding her ladder. I had the good fortune to appear on the QE2 and the food and dining were out of this world. They set me a single table every night and I had to wear a suit and a black tie. After every course the waiter, wearing white gloves, came to the table to brush off the crumbs with a small dust pan and brush. Some nights he brushed before I had finished eating so I strangled him with my black tie and was thrown out of the restaurant. Another evening he served me with a bottle of wine. (I could only afford the house at £32 a bottle), I knocked the bottle off the table and some of it splashed onto a lady in a backless dress on the table next to me. She stood up and I apologised whilst the waiter and I rubbed her down with a soggy wine-stained 100 per cent Irish linen serviette. (What else would you expect on the QE2?) The restaurant manager came to see what the fuss was about and joined in with the rubbing. I explained what had happened and asked him to forward the cleaning bill for the lady's dress. He said he'd once spilt red wine over his suit and unfastened his coat button to show me he was wearing an Armani suit costing over £500. I undid my suit jacket and showed him my label – Asda George £29.95. Obviously never having heard of Asda, he touched the material of my jacket, said, 'Good price. ' and continued rubbing down the lady who was by then sitting in her bra and pants waiting for course number eight.

I spent a lot of time in my cabin which was two strides to the left and four to the right. I had a bunk bed, a table, a chair and a shower. It was all very compact and shipshape. In fact, I could lie in bed, have a shower and read a book in the chair, all at the same time. A 40 watt bulb lit the cabin and with no porthole and positioned at the bottom of the ship, I could relate to the third class passengers from days gone by who were stuck below deck with not even a cabin steward to make them a swan from a towel. Going across the Atlantic Ocean from Southampton to New York in January through a force nine gale and waves of twenty feet is not my idea of cruising. Not having a porthole I couldn't see the waves, apart from when I sneaked out of my cabin on an evening to throw up over the side. (You have to make sure it's the right side, otherwise you see your dinner again if the wind is blowing in the wrong direction.) I would sit with the other passengers who had seasickness and we would discuss what would be the best cure. Some passengers wear tight wrist bands as this supposedly stops your circulation to the heart. (This stops sea sickness as you die). Other people prefer anti-seasickness pills and take them with a port and brandy. This I found to work as after six of these you don't give a shit about the pills. Some passengers are so sick they go to the ship's doctor and bare their buttocks for a prick up the bottom at a cost of £100 a shot. I don't advise this if your cabin steward is around because for the price of a chocolate and your head in the pillow he'll do it for nothing!

Those familiar with cruising, hopefully will laugh and relate to all this valid information and for those who have never been 'Hello Sailor' here's some more. After arriving on board you have to go through the lifeboat drill. This is the nautical law at sea and every passenger on board has to take part and muster at the assembly stations allocated. The ship's crew are positioned strategically to help you find your way to your lifeboat in the light of day or the dark of night. Seven bells ring in your cabin and through the ship and this is the ship's alarm. (Some passengers think it's the dinner bell and proceed to the restaurant in their evening dresses and black tie to eat once again.) Seven bells is actually the drill and you put on your lifejacket in the cabin and make your way to the muster station. Now, to watch passengers in a cabin try to don their lifejackets with straps to cross over left and right and tie a knot at the side in a room no bigger than a skip is similar to watching pensioners at a Christmas party doing the hokey cokey. In my eight foot square cabin, lifting the life jacket down from my single wardrobe positioned behind my table and above my bunk I could just about slip it over my head without putting one leg into the shower and falling arse over tit! These life jackets are bulky and are not to be blown up until you hit the water. They are bright orange and you can imagine three thousand passengers all lined up in these things on the deck of a ship looking like a Spanish orange grove waiting to be picked. The organisation is very good though and pensioners in wheel chairs and mobility frames are thrown over the side because they would take up extra room in the lifeboat. Once the crew have checked all cabins, passengers are made to stand on deck for thirty minutes, shivering and turning blue with the cold. They are then instructed to return to their cabins and also told that this drill can be repeated anytime, any place in the next few days. Some passengers, after watching Titanic in the cinema are so hung up about a ship's disaster they spend the rest of the cruise sitting in a lifeboat to get a seat! For the passengers who do love an adventure and thankfully, there are some who like a wander on shore to enjoy the experience of different cultures, there is the opportunity to discover new places.

Chapter 20

Wandering Ashore

Discovering is the best part of cruising for me. Without cruising I would never have been to New York, Cuba, the Cayman Islands, the Caribbean, up the Amazon, Brazil, Norway and The Isle of Wight. I've been left stranded at airports where fog and snow delayed flights to destinations where I had to meet a cruise ship in two days. I've landed in the middle of the night in airports like Aruba in the Caribbean where the runway was a cattle grid

I've passed over the Sahara desert where there's more sand than Blackpool beach and Lawrence gave us a wave after he he'd mounted his camel (well, in the desert you can't be choosy.)I've seen towns up the Amazon in the rain forests where the whole village gathers around a 1945 wartime radio in a corrugated tin roof hut listening to The Archers. I've seen families living in long open fishing boats with only blue plastic sheeting used as a canopy to protect them from the rain. I've seen street carnivals in Brazil with laughter, singing, dancing and celebrations lasting for over three days, with pig roasts in the streets and everyone happy apart from the pig. I've been in the Cayman Islands where fifty yards from the beach, jewellers' shops were selling white gold for $10.000 to American tourists whilst in the sea, fisherman were spearing fish, cutting it up on a marble slab on the beach and selling it to locals for fifty cents to make fish soup. What a contrast – the rich and the poor all within fifty yards of each other. The fisherman explained to me that if he could move up the beach he would get a job in a jeweller's shop selling gold and 'fuck the fish'!

Havana, the capital of Cuba, is something else and I loved the people and the place. The buildings are from the days of French Colonialism, three or four storeys high with ornate balconies, wrought

135

iron windows and beautiful architecture. That was before the days of communism. I last visited several years ago when the buildings, now in deterioration, housed people squatting in cardboard boxes and hanging their washing on the balconies. Begging is rife, and mothers send their children and toddlers on the streets to clasp the hands of tourists and ask for milk. I got off the ship and immediately outside the docks a wide boy offered his services for 25$ a day to stop the beggars harassing me. I said for 25$ a day I would do my act and nobody would harass me. He agreed and escorted me around Havana, showing me the tourist spots and sights. If you don't work in Cuba the Government pays you around £40 a month to survive and this is not cash but government coupons. People then have to spend these coupons in government stores in exchange for goods. Everyone is crowded into a shop full of boxes with only one person on the till; a line of people queuing to buy salami and cheese next to a garden hose, all on the same counter. Just like Lidl!

The Havana cigar is the best in the world and half the population work on the tobacco plantations. When the tobacco leaf is picked it is then rolled on the thigh of an eighteen year old Cuban girl before it is made into a cigar. Now, as you can imagine, this takes a lot of rolling and this girl has to be swapped every two days for another one because her thighs have gone brown and covered in nicotine and tourists visiting the factory keep asking her for a light. This hinders her job, especially when visitors want to take pictures of the cigars being rolled. On one occasion, an American tourist got so close between her legs with his camera, and just as he was about to click, he got poked in the eye as she was knocking out five King Edwards!

Norway was wonderful, especially to witness glacier mountains coming straight out the sea in front of your eyes. I could not believe the beauty of the country. However, Norway was one of the most expensive countries in the world that I visited. At the airport I paid £27.00 for a small coke and a slice of pizza. I paid £16.00 for a lager and realised I'd spent £43.00. That was £17 over my £26 daily budget. I phoned John

Ainsley and told him of my now carefree attitude towards money and he said he was still managing on £13 a day. The children had gone into care and his wife was doing Ann Summers parties with Lynda selling multi coloured condoms and vibrators; mail order (and there were a lot of male orders).

I loved to see the world and people watch and spent most of my time alone, apart from show time at 10 p.m. when you need to turn on and become funny. Entertainers and performers spend most of their lives sitting in cars, cabins or waiting at airports hour after hour in dressing rooms, pacing corridors with nerves before the dreaded hour, and questioning, 'Will they like me?' They travel thousands of miles a year up and down the motorways, stopping for a cheese sandwich and coffee at a motorway service station and getting change of 60p from a £20 note. They walk around strange towns in the rain at teatime when everyone is going home and they have to sit in the front window of a McDonalds with a burger, waiting for the venue to open at 7 p.m. before show time at 10 p.m. I have waited all my life. I should have been a waiter.

I eventually came back off the cruises which I did two or three times a year for five years and also continued working up and down the country. I was by now plodding along and really quite disillusioned with the business. I had seen comedians come through the ranks very quickly and attain overnight success with television appearances. I had been on the television once (trying to get the budgie off the curtains), I'd done extra work for BBC, Yorkshire and Granada, I'd mixed with the stars but never shone myself. I never got the chance to do my comedy on television and decided by now, after twenty five years in the business, my style and old school variety had come and gone. Summer seasons at the end of the pier were slowly disappearing, clubland was drying up and you had to have television exposure to put bums on seats in theatres. I had exposed my bum many times in theatres and this could be the reason why I never got on. Where was I going now? From here to Spain on holiday with Lynda, that's where.

Chapter 21

On the Costa Del Sol

We had friends on The Costa Del Sol and visited them on holiday. They lived near Benalmadena, Marbella and Malaga. This was the Crook's Paradise of southern Spain, where English bank robbers, thieves and the retired Arthur Daleys of this world had bought luxurious villas and properties, tax free. Some were escaping the law; others were the law and held the Spanish police, Lord Mayors, town planning architects and Government officials in the palms of their hands with bribes and payments in order to stay in Spain. Our friends were the Bonny and Clyde of Hull and had retired to Spain after robbing post offices, car boot sales and Oxfam shops. They were wanted by Saga and Shearing's holidays for stopping coaches and stealing packed lunches. They broke up tea dances and stole mobility chairs from overweight pensioners riding up and down the paseo, leaving them legless, with their carrier bags full of duty free fags and booze.

After several visits there, back and forth with a rowing boat full of contraband, from Hull and up the River Humber, across the North Sea, we decided to look at a club/restaurant in Los Boliches next door to Fuengirola on the coast. Why? I hear you ask – not again! Don't do it. Haven't you learned your lesson yet? Apparently not. The venue was called 'The Riverside' and had a circular marble bar in the middle of the room which could seat twenty people. There was a stage for cabaret and a small dance floor with steps to a seating area that could seat seventy people. The place was carpeted and decorated in green and pink and there was a stage lighting box with all its equipment and also a fitted kitchen. The venue was very impressive and Lynda and I both liked it. We were told it needed good management and had only been a white elephant because the owners didn't have the skills to run it. The owners were English and apart from The Riverside they owned a video shop, ships chandlers, a sailing yacht and a beautiful penthouse suite. They wined and dined Lynda and me on several occasions and we struck up a mutual friendship as well as interest in the business. By now you will have realised that I lived in a fantasy make believe world of always seeing positive and thinking 'I can make our lives better by trying once again.' Without the greatest of luck, my career as a comedian would always stay the same, and now after twenty five years in the business, nothing was going to change. I have always looked for some kind of security to go hand in glove with show business and was still ambitious to find success one way or another.

Spain and its coast was everything you could have wished for and together with the weather and way of life it looked like another adventure was on the horizon. Nothing ventured, nothing gained so with the blessings of relatives and friends, especially Bonnie & Clyde from Hull who needed a hideout, we negotiated a price to lease the venue over four years and put £20.000 down as a deposit. I had another great idea; we would operate as a cabaret/restaurant with singing waiters! Lynda agreed that she would chef and little Joey would come and work for us. Little Joey was now twenty and, similar to his father, was looking for new prospects and a change of life in the sun. Joey had worked in the hotel and catering business and was familiar with the skills of the profession and would run the bar, juggling cocktails and possibly Spanish women. Both Joey and Simon had the technical skills for mixing and producing music. Joey would also DJ as his brother had years ago at JOJO's. Simon, seeing common sense, had had a vision one night and had joined the banking industry back home. He was a clever lad and like his mum, could adapt himself to many things. I only did one thing – make people laugh – so combine this with excellent food on the Costa Del Sol and maybe this time we were onto a winner?

There was nothing like this place on the coast. There were plenty of small bars with entertainment run by retired coalminers from Barnsley but nowhere that provided a meal and a cabaret show in a lovely setting for the English holiday maker. This was the idea. In England, up and down the country I had met up with boys and girls on holiday park entertainment teams who I spoke to about the idea before we moved there. It was young people's dreams to come and work in Spain and to sing and dance. These kids were then performing at Pontin's and had the entertainment skills I was looking for. They all had personality too and I looked forward to them completing the team. As well as singing, they would wait the tables and serve food and help Lynda and me to make a success of this place. We organised a starting date for them to travel out to Spain when the venue was ready for opening. I honoured my bookings back home and Lynda and I rented out our house in England to keep some security if and when we wanted to return in the future. The date was set and in 1999 we travelled from Dover to Calais in our little Fiat car packed to the roof, with a great deal of apprehension and excitement. What would the future hold?

Chapter 22

The Talk of the Coast

We rented an apartment in Fuengirola, a tiny two bedroom place, very Spanish. There was a main wrought iron door into an entrance where we climbed the stairs to our apartment. Some apartments had small balconies where people kept their bikes, rubbish and potted plants and put their washing out. Air conditioning units stood off the wall like white fridges. However, the place was clean and would do for now as we thought this would be only the first apartment we would live in. I also had to find places for the 'singing waiters' to live when they arrived.

We met the owners and after paying our deposit, together with agreed terms and conditions, started work on revamping The Riverside into 'The Talk of the Coast,' our name for the new cabaret/restaurant. We gave ourselves three weeks to get the place shipshape and ready to open. Because we arrived in Spain in our Fiat, all our other possessions we decided to bring with us were coming from Hull in a van. This included the drum kit which I used in my act, a pa system for on stage and a little bit of furniture to make us feel at home. When this van arrived after seven days travelling, the contents were badly damaged as they had not been secured well enough to cross the North Sea. They had slid about in the van through France and Spain. When they reached us it looked like someone had thrown a bomb into a car boot sale. We collected our 'bits and pieces' – literally and glued them back together. I knocked the dints out of my drums and Lynda nailed the furniture back together.

In the meantime we had publicity printed and editorial features in the local Costa del Sol paper. Posters and flyers were distributed to surrounding businesses and shops and I walked the streets giving out

141

leaflets. The front of the building was painted and a new logo and advertising fascia boards graced the outside. It looked great. The singing waiters were coming in a week and I still had to find them accommodation, and then when they arrived, we needed to rehearse our stage songs and show them how to wait. Lynda prepared new menus and had all the doors and windows open in the kitchen to combat the thirty degrees of heat. This was February; the heat would get to forty degrees in June and July. Chickens would cook themselves in that heat without sitting in the oven. You could cook a full English breakfast on the bonnet of your car. That would save on electricity but what about the mess? Runny eggs, beans and bacon, flapping from side to side as you tried to wash up using your screen washers. No, we would stick to cooking inside with Lynda losing a stone a week from spending eight hours a day in the kitchen. If anybody (and I mean anybody) needs to lose weight, go to work in forty degrees of heat in a kitchen six days a week and that will stop you eating. Your appetite dwindles to nothing as the sweat runs down the back of your neck, past your back, down your legs and into your flipflops while you squelch around on the tile floor crushing the cockroaches that live on the premises. We didn't have many in the building because Lynda would feed them outside. They had a small table on the street and their own menu. Some days they couldn't get a table because the mosquitoes and ants had got there first. Non-paying customers already.

Our venue was situated in the village of Los Boliches and the continuation of Fuengirola, the large Spanish city on the south coast. We were five minutes from the sea and paseo and twenty minutes from Benalmadina on the coast road which ran towards Cadiz and Algiers. This was a time for development and we were surrounded by new multi storey apartment blocks with white wall balconies. There were dozens of cranes on building sites, towering in the sky with great arms ready to pick up anything and anybody that got in their way. The foundations of these buildings left a lot to be desired and occasionally you might see the odd Turkish, Spanish or Moroccan builder putting in four hours work before a siesta in the afternoon. How these apartments ever got finished I will never know. Some of them never did and buildings would stand half whitewashed with a breeze block and scaffolding base on a piece of land still displaying bricks, concrete and rubble, with water spilling out of open pipes. To make things more colourful, wild dogs and cats would live on these sites because in Spain they roam freely. The coast was bustling with business and Russian money was invested in properties right along the coast. The Costa Del Sol has thousands of English people living there and many bars became the homes and businesses of retired middle aged people who took early redundancy money for a life in the sun, a full English and fool's paradise. If only they had known the 'fools' part of the phrase was the most significant!

Malaga airport would have eight to ten flights per day from Birmingham, London, East Midlands, Liverpool and Leeds with 250 people per flight flocking to the Costa Del Sol every day of the week. That's 2,500 holiday makers a day just to Southern Spain. Estate agents greeted every flight with brochures and leaflets, enticing visitors to buy or rent businesses and properties in the sun. They would wait like vultures to sell to the gullible holidaymakers with pockets full of money, wanting to change their lives. Bars and restaurants were bought for cash or leased and for a cash deposit you could be serving your first pint of Carlsberg and a full English breakfast in three weeks.

We greeted our staff of singing waiters including our son Joey, and their excitement and enthusiasm was overwhelming as they settled down into the apartments I had found them. Once again, to keep costs down, these apartments were quite minimal, very Spanish and part of large apartment blocks. We spent a week learning and rehearsing the show and trying on waiters' sparkly waistcoats, learning to pull pints and carry food. We advertised on the beaches in full costume while singing, and a couple of the boys went on roller skates distributing leaflets along the promenade.

Our team of six people had worked twelve hours a day to promote the venue over the last three weeks and at last, we were set to open. We opened our doors for the public to come. They were a mixture of British expats, English business people who we had invited with their friends and some Spanish guests inquisitive to see what 'this new place' was all about. It was still early March so we invited the donkeys off the beach, the wild cats and dogs from the building sites, the Moroccan and Turkish drug dealers, the Spanish street pickpockets and any old ladies over the age of ninety dressed in black with sun dried wrinkled faces.

The opening night was a great success. The English mixed with the Spanish and the singing waiters sang and served food while I performed my comedy show in four languages: (Geordie, Scouse, Welsh and Brummie). Well, we were now international and audiences were coming from all over the world. The Spanish enjoyed our hospitality and danced the flamenco to 'The Birdie Song', led by two KGB men from Moscow, a hit man and a Turk in a fez who did an impression of Tommy Cooper. Prams and kids would be pushed through the front door, their families from as far afield as Rochdale and Warrington, looking for a full English breakfast. Well, I'm afraid we didn't open until the evening. We were a restaurant cabaret venue so they were sent down the paseo to the English greasy spoons where they could sample bacon, beans and fried bread and a pint of lager at 9.00 am in the morning – a bit like Wetherspoons. An Englishman abroad never changes! This was March, remember, so until May, 75% of our customers would be residents living on the coast, along with a handful of holiday makers who tried the door, expecting a fry up. We had planned the venue as an evening celebration of good food and entertainment and slowly, as word got around, people from all walks of life came. Yes, we could honestly say that everyone from bank robbers to crooks, everyone graced our venue. Mid weeks in March we were very quiet and some nights we would work to only ten people.

Weekends were busy however, and we catered for parties, celebrations and the odd company night out.

One evening when it was quiet I noticed water trickling through the tiles of the seating area floor. I took a brush and swept the water away. This returned on several occasions and was very off putting to diners as they tucked into their tapas and gambas pil pil (prawns in a piri piri sauce) with water around their ankles. Upon further investigation and detective work from inside the apartments above the restaurant, we discovered this happened when the tenants above our building flushed their toilets. The sewerage was coming down pipes through our dining room and along the floor. This was because the sewerage pipes were not wide enough to take the effluence of around forty apartments above, all pulling their chains at night. The system had never been modernised so the sewerage couldn't clear itself to the drain outside so came back down the pipe and under our dining room floor. Now, this would only happen if the Spanish tenants were feeling 'flush' together and the result would rise above our restaurant floor. At first it looked just like water until after mopping and ringing out the evidence, we realised this was 'Spanish poo'! Because we had mood lighting and candles on the tables to create atmosphere I started to walk discreetly around with a mop and bleach, scrubbing and wiping the affected area. One Sunday morning, a Spanish bank holiday, the floor was in such a mess I called a tanker company to put a large pipe down the drain outside to clean the shit from inside. Until this problem was dealt with the diners would have to sit in wellingtons and life jackets with pegs on their noses.

Now this was the situation. It was a Spanish holiday, everyone was religious and at church and I was looking for a sewerage tanker on a Sunday morning to come and empty our sewer and the only appropriate word in Spanish I knew was 'El-crappo'. After spending an hour on a Spanish phone trying to talk to someone who couldn't understand broad Yorkshire I was told that for £100, a tanker would come as soon as possible. But 'as soon as possible' in Spanish could be 'manana' (tomorrow), next week or Christmas! After more swilling of the floor, more mop buckets and banging on apartment doors asking people not to have a piss or shit mid-afternoon, the tanker arrived and sucked the effluence from the creaking drain, now relieved to be emptied. We cleaned and cleaned and made the tables and chairs ready for the evening diners with a main course special 'TURD IN THE HOLE'. You couldn't make this up, could you? Well, I'm not and as you've probably guessed, the adventure went sadly from bad to worse.

With the flushing of the apartments and costs outweighing takings we were becoming drained of money and living from week to week. The service, food and shows were excellent but I now wondered if I'd wanted to attract a market which wasn't there. I approached the coach companies, including Thomson's holidays, for nights out but they didn't encourage trips outside their hotels because their revenue in bar takings would suffer. Hotels kept their guests in their hotels with house entertainment such as flamenco shows. Our venue was not for families so we didn't have any customers from holiday parks. The owner of the venue came several times to a night out and assured me that business would get better as we got into summer but this didn't happen. By April all our takings were spent on rent, food, and staff wages. We asked if the rent could be reduced as I was now having sleepless nights worrying about paying bills and the drains weren't much better. When I complained to the owner about the circumstances he warned me he would take the club back and offer the lease for sale again. We had signed agreement papers but after questioning their validity we went to a Spanish lawyer who told us the papers were worthless and not legal in Spain. We had had our legs pulled once again.

After that, the owner changed the locks on the venue so we couldn't even gain entry. After more legal advice we broke into the restaurant and changed the locks back again. The owner then told me that although we had regained entry he wouldn't allow the premises to open the next week and threatened to physically close the place himself. This man weighed around eighteen stone so I didn't fancy fighting him in the doorway or the street. As luck had it, I'd met an acquaintance the week before who, after explaining my position, offered to ease the situation. Together with two of his pals they became our doormen for a week, armed discreetly with base-ball bats under the table. They called the owner up and told him they were ready to see him any time and had a table waiting for him. He never came. We took him to a Spanish court and found out he had never owned the premises and was himself leasing the property from a Spanish landlord in Madrid. He was sub-contracting to us, trying to make money on the property and the genuine owners knew nothing about us. His arrangements or his so called 'legal' agreements, which he'd drawn up himself, were issued to anyone he'd managed to persuade to rent or lease the venue. We presumed he had done this before as he was ordered to return our £20,000 deposit less costs and the venue was closed. The staff went back to England and another chapter of our lives had closed.

As I write this, I feel the sadness and despair we went through in those months of trying once again to make something happen that was impossible. It never could have worked. The idea was good, the location bad – just off the main paseo and not in view. That is why it had failed in the past and without a lot of sustainable money thrown at it for another year it could not survive. All around the area a lot of beautiful restaurants stood empty every night with staff and chefs standing in the doorways waiting for custom. We always wondered how they survived but they didn't have to take money because the owners, like our 'owner' had many more important irons in the fire. Many restaurants and bars were only a front for laundering money. I always learn too late – I should have bought a laundry.

We had to wait for a period of a couple of months before the money was settled so after licking our wounds and paying off debts I went to do some shows on the coast to British holidaymakers in bars and hotels with Lynda doing a singing spot to open the show. At least we had an audience and there was no cooking for Lynda. The money paid to entertainers in Spain, Portugal and Greece is terrible so this was not a new career and was only seasonal. I did very well and the shows went excellently as our standard was higher than a fellow playing guitar, wearing a sombrero, clicking his heels and yodelling in Spanish. Or else a retired miner from Selby with dyed black hair and sideboards wearing an ill-fitting Elvis suit with his pot belly protruding through his string vest singing 'The Wonder of You! We suffered the consequences of setting up our pa equipment in the heat of the midday sun and taking it all out again to move to another venue the next day. Lynda also worked in hotels and kitchens and on leisure yachts and cruisers. She cleaned villas, boats, swimming pools and patio decking to earn the money we needed to stay afloat.

We continued with this work for around two months and when our money was paid to us and cleared at the bank we decided to come back home to the house we'd rented out. A good job we had saved that one!

Lynda couldn't face the journey home in that Fiat stacked to the roof with our belongings so decided to fly home. I would do a Michael Palin, travelling alone across southern Spain, through the Pyrenees Mountains, into France and back to Calais – a three day adventure. Our pa equipment, drums and sticks of furniture would be packed once again in a lorry to be smashed to bits again. 'You never learn, do you?' said Lynda!

I travelled for those three days reading a map of France and Spain positioned on the driver's seat whilst steering a tiny car loaded up like the Clampetts' truck. I went up mountains through France and coasted along some of the most beautiful scenery in Europe travelling eight to twelve hours a day. On the first day at around 7 p.m. I stopped in a lovely hotel/restaurant in France and treated myself to a fabulous steak and a bottle of red wine. Exhausted, I then retired flat out in a lovely bedroom with a balcony and creeping ivy up the wall. I had a word with her and suggested she use the front door if she wanted to come in. Ivy never replied because she couldn't speak English so I closed the balcony windows and Ivy crept next door.

With the car coughing and spluttering I made it to Calais on the second day at around 6 p.m. and crossed over to Blighty and Dover, escaping back onto the English motorways and the familiarity of Yorkshire. After I shared my three day journey and travel experiences with Lynda she just said, 'Serves you right!' However, it was a lovely trip and after driving for thirty six hours it brought back all the memories of driving alone in this country over the past thirty years to 'earn a bob'.

Chapter 23

A Little Bit Extra

In 2001 I became an 'extra' – or what is now called 'a support or background artist' on television to supplement my income and I occasionally still do this. The description for the profession of an extra is 'Actor engaged temporarily as one of the crowd'. Well, I never wanted to be 'one of a crowd' but we're told what to do on a film set for a day's pay. This is what an 'extra' means – to earn extra money!

I joined a casting agency in Leeds, the ATS (Artists Theatrical Services) which supplied extras to Granada TV, Yorkshire TV and BBC Television for films, soaps, sit coms and dramas which were made in the North of England, shows such as *Brideshead Revisited, Harry's Game, In Loving Memory, The LadyKillers, Only When I Laugh, Last of the Summer Wine and Duty Free* and long running ones which are still on ITV such as *Emmerdale* and *Coronation Street*.

My claim to fame is mixing with the stars on such epics. Well, I say 'mixed'. I was once with Laurence Olivier, no less, in the makeup room of Granada TV Studios. He was sitting in the next chair and as he turned to get out of his seat he looked at me, said 'Shift!' and walked out of the door. On another occasion I sat next to Thora Hird in an episode of *In Loving Memory* in a cinema in Leeds. I had to hold the bucket seat down for her as she sat next to me. She was wearing a large bustle and carrying a rather cumbersome parasol. As we were waiting to shoot the scene she rummaged in her handbag, produces a period pillbox and proceeded to pop an assortment of pills into her mouth. I was suffering from hay fever at the time and blew a very loud and wet sneeze in her direction. 'Move him away from me!,' she demanded. 'He's full of germs! I can't catch a cold.' She then popped another three pills down her throat. Thora may have been a hypochdriac but she was also a true trouper and acted well into her eighties – with prominent shares in Boots the Chemist!

I was once in a TV period drama as a First World War soldier in the trenches. I had a basin put on my head to have a haircut and looked like Rowan Atkinson in the first series of *Blackadder.* At 6.30 am the makeup artists aren't as keen as they should be so to cut twenty or thirty extras' hair one after the other can leave a lot to be desired. We each received £14 extra for the haircuts and went on set in full uniform, with wadding, packs and guns. However, I spent the rest of the day under a blanket – dead! I wouldn't have minded but I had to work the clubs on a night for the next two months with that ridiculous haircut!

An extra's life as portrayed by Ricky Gervais in his very funny TV show was actually characterised more colourfully and less demeaning than in real life. For instance, in the staff canteen or at the outdoor catering unit on a television set, extras can't eat until the principal actors, camera crew, lighting, makeup, drama queens and Uncle Tom Cobley and All have been fed and watered. So in a line of fifty people or so with only an hour's break, sometimes all there was left to eat was a broken Jacob's cream cracker! There was, and still is, a pecking order right through the ranks of television, just as in the famous Ronnie Barker and John Cleese sketch: 'I know my place'. I was always at the end of the line when they were dishing out food, compliments and gold stars.

On several occasions I was in trouble for making the cast and extras laugh on set when it was totally unacceptable. I remember years ago standing in Rita's cabin in *Coronation Street* when she was doing a scene with Mavis. I was told to be in the background, thumbing through magazines. I was so busy looking at the books, swopping them around, picking up newspapers and moving them from shelf to shelf, the director stopped the scene and said, 'Stop that extra from being so bloody busy!' Well, I thought it was the only chance I'd get to be noticed and get as close as I could to the stars but I was nearly sent home. It was like school; you're told to get your coat off the peg in the cloakroom and leave.

Another time I was on the set of *Emmerdale*, sitting opposite and talking to another extra at a table in The Woolpack. You're told to mime to each other to simulate conversation so you're not picked up by the microphone but not to distract the principal actors from their parts. On the word, Action! the other extra started to mime his words and I mimed back, 'What?' He continued miming and I repeated' What?' with a grin on my face. He tried a third time then I mouthed, 'Sorry, I can't hear you' and started to display gestures, such as holding my hand to my ear, to convey my reply. Well, I cracked up and the scene was stopped. To my dismay, he went straight to the studio floor manager and complained that I was trying to make him laugh and spoil his acting. 'After all,' he said, 'It may be a joke to Joey Howard but this a career for me'. I was suitably warned. I didn't see my co-extra again until about a year later when I visited Alton Towers. He was playing Grandma in *Little Red Riding Hood.* He remembered me with obvious contempt but I showed no bad feeling. I told him I was pleased to see that he was working and 'keeping the wolf from the door'. Not a titter!

Earlier this year I enquired about extras work again and found to my surprise a date was fixed for a day's work on *Coronation Street* in February. It had been a few years since I had visited this world famous set and travelled to Salford Quays in Manchester. A building the size of a football stadium has been built entirely for The Street. This includes the set itself with the houses, shops, factory, builder's yard, The Rover's Return and bistro. There are also indoor studio sets, workshops, administration, restaurant and parking for the hundreds of people who work exclusively on this programme.

On arrival at Salford Quays by tram or bus it takes around twenty minutes to walk around the building to the entrance which is guarded like Buckingham Palace with security ramps, terrorist blocks and barriers with security guards. There are CCTV cameras and a password to get in. The password changes daily from Ena Sharples to Albert Tatlock! Once within the walls of the inner sanctum you report to reception and are frisked for weapons by Gail Tilsley and Tyrone Dobbs and then given an ID badge to go to the extras room where the part time 'lovies' are dwelling on past experiences of the programmes they have 'starred in' over the years.

That day, after waiting around for three hours I was called onto the famous cobbled street to walk past Bill Roach (Ken Barlow) as he was shooting an outdoor scene, talking to an actor in the doorway of The Cabin. Now, Ken is the longest serving actor in The Street – over fifty years in total – and he is looked after liked Donald Trump.

Outside on location can be very cold on a February afternoon in Manchester with the damp Mancunian air clinging to the torso of a extra's body wearing only a shirt and jumper to give the impression it's Easter! With a spot of occasional rain and seeing your breath, one isn't prepared for how long this scene will take under the director's guidance. Some directors can do a dozen takes if necessary, just for two minutes of dialogue and prolong the agony of hyperthermia for another thirty minutes.

Now the crew, make up, lighting, sound and Tom Dick & Harry are prepared for these long days in The Street. After all, they do it every day and dress like they were filming *Scott of the Antarctic*. Layers of jumpers, woolly hats, padded anoraks, fur lined boots, scarves, gloves and thick socks are the order of the day. The extras stand freezing in their spring attire, me included. We are not gifted with such luxuries as make up or hairdressers so although the scene is supposed to be Spring, the director doesn't want to see glowing red faces caused by a biting north wind or us blowing snot bubbles from running noses. Extras are kept at a distance so you can't see them shivering!

Ken Barlow could be out there for quite awhile so every three minutes between shots, the wardrobe mistress brings him a full length fur lined waterproof coat and repeatedly puts it on him and take it off between takes. Bill Roach, who is now in his eighties, doesn't feel the cold and his beautiful head of hair is combed and lacquered as often as his coat is taken on and off. After all, Ken has stood out there for over fifty years so he deserves the treatment and the pandering. While this is going on, we're going bluer and bluer as we are huddled together to create a crowd scene. By now, most of us aren't bothered anymore about being seen on camera and just want to hide in the middle of the crowd to keep warm. We are then sent back into the extras' room to huddle together around a one bar fire, drink tea and wait for the next scene to take place.

Three weeks later I eagerly watched the episode sitting on the settee at home. I turned around to buff up a cushion and missed my appearance!

That's show business for an extra. One minute you're there and the next minute you're not!

Chapter 24

From Spain to Rain

On returning from Spain to rain I had to pick up the pieces and start again. After being abroad for a year you lose your contacts and are not flavour of the month anymore. This was now 1999 I had no work to go back to, apart from being 'an extra' again. I considered hiring donkeys on Blackpool beach; you can hire them because they have a little nut under the saddle! I could have been a Punch and Judy man but Lynda wouldn't move to Blackpool and live in a small striped tent on the sand. She did favour hitting me with a bat every day but pointed out she could do that in Newport where we returned to our little rented house.

However, I did go to the seaside – to Blackpool and somehow got work at the Metropole Hotel which stands on the front. I say 'stands', this place was now on its knees; it groaned from the iron and rust supporting it. After twenty five years of neglect it badly needed a refurbishment and a paint job. It attracted the same clientele; people on their knees covered in rust on walking frames and mobility scooters, dressed in caps and shell suits. This was to be my summer audience for the next twenty years. Pensioners used to dress in fifty shades of beige, macks and rain mates; not any more – these were retired gladiators of the benefit system. They belonged to the over fifteen stone club who could drink and smoke most people under the table and still consume three meals a day, followed by fish and chips or a kebab at 11 p.m. They played bingo in the hotel and on Blackpool front for four hours a day, in between drinking six pints of lager and threatening the donkeys with a ride.

They would come from all over Yorkshire, Lancashire, the Midlands and the North East on coach trips costing £50 – £60: Monday to Thursday. These holidays served tinned soup, shepherd's pie and semolina thrown in. The tables were set in rows similar to a prison canteen. Bingo would follow the meal, plus cabaret provided by the likes of yours truly or a singer accompanied by an organist and drummer who also would play for strict tempo dancing. Usually, the musicians had seen better days themselves and wearing crumpled dinner jackets and moth eaten bow ties would take to the stage and entertain the audience with everything from The Saint Bernard's waltz to Viva Espana. Twenty four games of bingo would follow, accompanied by gin and tonics that the women smuggled into the ballroom in their handbags. This tipple put them into a party atmosphere, ready for a laugh and a little cheek from me who would play this gig once a week for the rest of the year. Two years later the place caught fire and was gutted. They say the fire did £25 worth of damage!

I also got work in Eastbourne for a national coach company. I wouldn't say their guests were old but the local funeral parlour had NEXT on the door. I toured for this company for fifteen years, working in Ilfracombe, Weymouth, Scarborough, Devon, Bournemouth and the Lake District, doing three shows a week and once again, travelling the length and breadth of England. Sometimes I would witness a death on the dance floor as an eighty three year old male would try and lift his seventy six year old lover to the climax move in Dirty Dancing. Or someone would have a stroke after the excitement of winning a £10 full house on the bingo; or maybe choking in the dining room after trying to poke down another helping of corn beef hash!

Holiday Parks were another source of income. Once again, pensioners from April to the summer holidays, and then six weeks of families running riot on these colossal sites. Eight hundred people were fed chicken nuggets and jelly and ice cream in two sittings in dinner halls the size of football fields. I hated the summer holidays with the families. They walked about, pushed prams and played the machines in the amusements whilst I performed. Men would stand at the bar jeering whilst the kids danced to my jokes on the dance floor. I couldn't wait to get back to the pensioners when schools went back after the summer. At least they would listen for twenty minutes before nodding off or having to be taken to the loo and toileted.

The nicer work was for the Warner's Hotels and I worked all their thirteen sites for these fifteen years. I also played to adult audiences at venues such as stately homes, country manors and hotel listed buildings. Warner's was like cruising on land for people who didn't like the sea or flying. They offered first class food, restaurants, health Spa and purpose built cabaret rooms for entertainment, wining and dining. You could see Joey Howard on a Friday at Warner's and Lulu, Jane McDonald or Russell Watson on the Saturday and maybe Ronnie Corbett or Brian Connelly on the Sunday. I performed before all these top TV entertainers and got standing ovations. In fact, the audiences were still standing as these stars left the stage and I walked on. What a triumph! Joking apart, they were fabulous venues and I still perform some of them today when comedy is required.

Between 2011–2014 I got the opportunity to do a twenty week summer season near home, at The Spa Theatre Scarborough, entertaining family audiences and coach loads of pensioners looking forward to nostalgia and seaside fun (and sometimes, looking for somewhere to keep out of the rain and wind coming from the North Sea). Through the six week summer holidays I also played to kids with ants and sand in their pants, fidgeting until the intermission when they could fill their little faces with ice cream and sugar drinks. These made them super hyper and they would run up and down the aisles, in between playing on their mobile phones. Sometimes, however, the kids would actually enjoy the shows. Apart from pantomime, some of them would never have seen live entertainment in that environment. They enjoyed the lights, the music, the costumes and the ambience. It's a magical world of make believe; they could be carried along with song, dance and comedy, the same as we were as kids when we went to

Joey Who?

Saturday morning pictures, such as the ABC Minors, to see Roy Rogers, Flash Gordon and Laurel and Hardy. We flicked lolly sticks at the screen and tried to throw our best friends off the balcony and into the stalls. People's leisure time has changed; what makes people laugh has changed; comedy has changed. But one of the biggest thrills for an entertainer is when a family brings their young children into the foyer of the theatre to see you after the show, waiting in line for an autograph or to buy a DVD.

Scarborough had put on a variety show for many years and at that time would attract hundreds of people on holiday wanting to see their television favourites at the seaside. This was the same in Blackpool, Skegness, Great Yarmouth, Bournemouth and all the major seaside towns that attracted thousands of visitors. To see Les Dawson, Little & Large, Ken Dodd, Cannon& Ball, Tommy Cooper all headlining shows, supported by dancing girls and singers, jugglers and a band in the pit, was a great family night out and brought live entertainment to the masses. These and other top comedians with shows on television took box office records year after year. If a TV attraction like Cannon & Ball could get a summer season from June to September, then a pantomime and cabaret plus a theatre tour, with a television series for good measure, they never stopped working.

The general working class public, apart from working five days a week, going to a football match on a Saturday and the working men' s clubs on a Friday, Saturday and Sunday and a week at the seaside in the summer, didn't seem to want much more. Before the advent of the package holiday to Spain our pleasures were simple. Before computers, technology and mobile phones, the working man enjoyed his live entertainment with a pint and a pie to go with it. Apart from the clubs on the corner of your street, and there were hundreds (I know, I played nearly all of them) a trip to Batley Variety Club or The Fiesta in Sheffield or Stockton was a treat, with chicken in a basket, in a two thousand seated cabaret room. To watch acts such as Shirley Bassey,

Chapter 24: From Spain to Rain

Neil Sedaka, Gene Pitney, Freddie Starr or Bob Monkhouse was a nightly experience and these venues were full every night. I supported The Searchers, Lulu, Cannon & Ball and Gene Pitney on their sell out weekly shows in several popular venues.

Men would put on their £12 best suits from Burton's and women their best frocks. A coach would be arranged from all over the North for a special night out. Today you go to the theatre or a stadium to watch your favourite acts. In those days the only time you went to the theatre was to have your tonsils out and the stadium to watch greyhound racing. A new breed of entertainment was hatched and the old mould was broken. Ben Elton came, the comedy clubs came, with French & Saunders, Rick Mayall, and Eddie Izzard. Rowan Atkinson came from college, along with Richard Curtis and they became alternative mainstream. Variety became a forgotten word, a dinosaur and out of fashion. The whole variety show business industry went into decline.

Seaside shows suffered and without the star names, audiences didn't want feathers, tits and sparkle or has-been television comics telling jokes only your mum and dad laughed at. Audiences were getting younger and more sophisticated and some nights I found myself playing in a five hundred seater theatre in Scarborough to thirty or forty people smelling of liniment. People would ring up and say, 'What time does the show start?' and the box office would reply, 'What time can you get here?' We had a full cast of singers and dancers (and me, the sole comedian). We performed show pieces from shows such as Les Miserables, West Side Story and Blues Brothers with full costumes, production and lighting. One night, all the lights fused and I went on with a candle and sung war songs from the Blackout. I asked the audience up onto the stage one by one as I knew their first names. I asked them if they would like to join in with Vera Lynn's 'Eskimo song' and a man shouted out, 'Not whale meat again!' The other dozen people in the audience waved their hankies. I did this theatre for three summers and we couldn't pull the public in. I stood outside with a gun and they still resisted.

Apart from the Cromer Pier Summer Variety Show which I played in 2017, the variety show has gone. In saying that, for the show at The Cromer Theatre, which has been going for over forty years, we played to eight hundred people a day and the audiences, young and old, loved every performance, two shows a day. Cromer is a lovely little seaside town and people come every year from Norfolk and Suffolk to watch variety. It is amazing and nowhere else in the country can compete with the success that this show has achieved all these years.

In 2018 (don't the pages fly by?) I was asked for the first time in my career to play a Dame in pantomime. I had only ever before dressed up as a woman in private for my close friends! So, after deeply considering for around three minutes, I decided to rise to the challenge and play the part of Nurse Flossy in Snow White & the Six Dwarfs (we were on a budget), at The Royal Theatre Lincoln for a six week Christmas Season.

As the oldest member of a large cast that included kids, actors, singers and dancers, I stepped tentatively into the fantasy world of pantomime. There were two teams of children playing dwarfs, the law only allowing children to work so many hours a week. Mothers chaperoning their children were in and out of the building, going to the loo with them every five minutes, never allowing these little people one minute out of their sight.

I was relegated to the basement, imprisoned behind a black curtain with my make-up: eight costumes, wigs, tights, jewellery and three different pairs of very expensive Doc Martens. As I stared at my reflection in an old cracked mirror, it blurred into the resemblance of a cross between my mother and father, both dressed in drag at one of my mother's Boxing Day get-togethers.

I had to arrive ninety minutes before curtain-up. It was a military operation getting my make-up on. The dressers and dancers alike were very patient until I got the hang of how to look like a Dame rather than a 'slapper'. In my case, the difference is subtle, hardly noticeable!

Some people are blessed with good looks but in my late sixties I have definitely been hit with the ugly stick. Make-up can't always camouflage, rather it highlights. I would have frightened Jack the Ripper down a dark alley. I was asked to make a personal appearance as Nurse Flossy at The Lincoln Children's Hospital for Christmas. The kids hid under the sheets and two nurses were given gas and air!

Some weeks we did thirteen shows and on certain days, three shows a day. After what seemed like endless choruses of the 'Baby Shark' song, shouting at audiences full of primary school kids, Scouts and Brownies, I realised that my career must have reached the pinnacle of exuberance. In the finale, after sixty three shows and over 400 changes of costume, I stepped onto the stage for the last time, dressed as a Christmas tree. It weighed over fifty kilos and was covered in sparkling lights. I sweated like a Sumo wrestler in a sauna. The fairy on the top had started to droop. I knew the feeling...

After that performance, I threw my under skirts, tights, jockstrap, knickers and bra to the floor, scrubbed the makeup from my face and Nurse Flossy was gone.

Come back Joey Howard. All is forgiven!

While I spent weeks at the seaside and pantomime trying to re-invent myself over the last few years, Lynda (remember her?) has gone from strength to strength. She went on to study at college and university for five years as a mature student and attained a degree in Psychology and Criminology. This gives you a hint that after trying to understand me, and the workings of a dreamer on cloud nine, she could have possibly got away with murdering me, cutting me up into little bits and serving me as stew when she was working as a cook in an old people's home in Goole. She has worked herself to the bone over the years and that's why on Halloween she doesn't hire fancy dress, she just goes as a skeleton!

Now, apart from analysing serial killers, singing in clubs, pop groups and dance bands, being a mother, wife, hairdresser, landlady, chef and university graduate, in 2013 Lynda decided to form her own theatre production company which was called The Mucking Fuddles. She wrote all the plays herself and acted in most of them. However, after realising that the work involved in getting her plays to production meant it took her away from what she loved doing best, she now concentrates on her writing and has become a commissioned and published writer. Lynda is also a proud member of Hull's collective 'Women of Words'. She still sings as well; recently headlining at the East Riding Theatre for She Productions with the girl band 'The Girlfriends' who began when they were sixteen and are all now in their seventies.

This means all her training as a cook, cleaner and domestic has gone to the wall and I have to live in filth and squalor as she has now become the famous one and I have taken a back seat. That's where she makes me sit in the car. What does subservient mean? However, she did let me occasionally write some comedy for her drama group which allowed me to present sketches to a new medium of theatregoers and the opportunity to share the stage with her as an actor.

So, that's show business – full of surprises and disappointments and as my father always said, "Take everything in life with a pinch of salt" (He made an awful cup of tea!). 'Why do I still do it?' I sometimes ask myself. 'Why have I done it all these years?' I can hear you asking me that. Well, if you have a natural talent, you will do it. Every opportunity to test my ability to make people laugh I grasp with both hands. The personal challenge to make people smile never leaves you. Charlie Chaplin wrote a song about it and he made millions 'Smile'. There is nothing more rewarding than receiving the approval and laughter from an appreciative audience.

Once a performer, always a performer...

Epilogue

So now the rain has stopped and you have killed two hours standing in this shop, reading my life story, I don't suppose you'll be buying the book. After all, what good is it to you now, apart from a door stop or draught excluder? So, I might as well go back on the shelf next to Joan Collins.

But, if you can wipe the dust off my cover and push me back, please just leave me protruding out a little so I can drop onto the floor. You never know, another book lover might pick me up and say, Oh look – JOEY WHO? – fifty per cent off – I'll have that!'

END